FROM FUGITIVE TO FREEDOM

FROM FUGITIVE TO FREEDOM

The Amazing Story of How a Holocaust Survivor Became a Nazi Hunter

JACK BOEKI &
ANNA-LEA BOEKI

FIREFLY BOOKS

A FIREFLY BOOK

Published by Firefly Books Ltd. 2026

First printing

Library of Congress Control Number: 2026940964

Library and Archives Canada Cataloguing in Publication
Title: From fugitive to freedom : the amazing story of how a Holocaust survivor became a Nazi hunter / Jack Boeki & Anna-Lea Boeki.
Names: Boeki, Jack, author. | Boeki, Anna-Lea, author.
Identifiers: Canadiana 20260191671 | ISBN 9780228106364 (softcover)
Subjects: LCSH: Boeki, Jack. | LCSH: Jews—Netherlands—Biography. | LCSH: Holocaust survivors—Netherlands—Biography. | LCSH: Intelligence officers—United States—Biography. | LCSH: Holocaust, Jewish (1939-1945)—Netherlands—Personal narratives. | LCGFT: Autobiographies. | LCGFT: Biographies. | LCGFT: Personal narratives.
Classification: LCC DS135.N6 B64 2026 | DDC 940.53/18092—dc23

Published in the United States by
Firefly Books (U.S.) Inc.
P.O. Box 1338, Ellicott Station
Buffalo, New York
14205

Published in Canada by
Firefly Books Ltd.
50 Staples Avenue, Unit 1
Richmond Hill, Ontario
L4B 0A7

Cover design: Hartley Millson
Interior design: Stacey Cho

Front cover and back cover photos courtesy of Jack Boeki

Printed in China | E

FSC
www.fsc.org
MIX
Paper | Supporting responsible forestry
FSC® C160794

We gratefully acknowledge the financial support of the Government of Canada for our publishing program.

We are grateful for the support of Yosef Wosk in our making Jack Boeki's story of his wartime experiences into this book.

I'm grateful to my loved ones, Claude, my CIC family,
and the kind strangers who helped me.

Homeless — May 10, 1940

The Germans broke their repeated promises to respect the neutrality of Holland and invaded my country on May 10, 1940. They sealed their conquest with a wholesale bombing attack on Rotterdam on May 14 at around one o'clock in the afternoon. Our home on the outskirts of the city. We were hiding in the basement and I can still see the fear on my father's face. The bombs were not landing on our house, but all around us. We could hear the bombs whistle as they fell, the sound piercing through our ears, then we felt the explosions reverberate in our chest as they shook the ground.

The place that had been my home was no more. The center of the city was destroyed by bombs. I was just weeks away from turning 16 and I can still smell the city smoldering, the rubble emitting a foul stench. Piles of broken bricks and stones buried the streets where buildings once stood. The firestorms that developed after the bombing made us homeless and without possessions. Gone were furniture, clothing, family heirlooms, paintings, art, jewelry, photographs, important documents, and souvenirs – everything had turned to ash.

CONTENTS

PART III

JOINING THE RESISTANCE

PART IV

FIGHTING BACK

PART V

AFTER THE WAR

PART I

FAMILY LIFE BEFORE THE WAR AND LIFE UNDER THE OCCUPATION

CHAPTER 1

My Family

I HAVE OFTEN wondered about my last name, Boeki. Despite being Dutch, my father looked Spanish and I myself have a very dark complexion. It made me wonder about my mysterious Spanish ancestry. As a child, I remember a large oil painting of my paternal grandmother in our home. I'm not sure why, but it kind of scared me. She was dressed as a Spanish noble with a typical black veil around her head. I hardly knew her, but I do remember visiting her in the hospital. One of my parents told me her leg had been amputated because she had diabetes. My young mind couldn't quite conceive such a thing, so my imagination invented that her missing leg was buried under the earth.

The Municipal Birth Registration of the City of Rotterdam lists the names of my forefathers going as far back as the 15th century. Prior to this, it seems that there were no records. The Spanish and Portuguese Inquisitions were rampant during that time, and I am sure that my father's ancestors came from that part of Europe and fled to Holland with the expulsion of Jews from Spain around 1492.

I was born in Rotterdam, Holland on May 31, 1924, in an apartment located at the corner of Tollensstraat and Noordmolenstraat. Below the apartment was the retail store my father, Jacob Boeki, had opened before I was born. The store became well known as "*Boeki van het hoeki*" which means Boeki on the Corner. In Dutch, Boeki means "little book," and it sounds a bit like the way we pronounce book in English, with the "*i*" meaning "little" which rhymes with the Dutch word for corner, "hoeki."

My father's store did not sell books, it sold electronic goods like batteries, wiring accessories and radios, as well as bicycle tires. My father manufactured the battery-operated radios and their batteries (which he named "Lea" after my sister) in a small workshop manned by three workers. He was one of the first in Holland to produce these huge radios and sell them in his store. By 1940, my father was operating seven stores in different locations in central Rotterdam.

I considered my father to be a handsome man. He was lanky and six feet tall. I know very little about his background. I vaguely remember hearing that he was trained as a butcher in his teens. This might have been true, because whenever he bought our meat from the butcher shop across the street from our apartment, he always told them exactly how to cut the portion he wanted. His father, Isaac Boeki, had died very young. Whether or not my father got to know him, I don't know; he never spoke about him. My paternal grandmother's name was Lena (or Leentje) Presburg. She remarried after her husband's death, but I know very little about the events of that time.

On December 23, 1914, my father married Leentje Berkelouw. I that my parents loved each other very much because they were very affectionate. I called her Mamma. She loved to make us laugh and she adored opera, her favorite being *La Traviata* by Verdi. She was a very strong woman who helped my father produce beautiful lampshades that he sold in his stores. She hired a team of seamstresses to wrap the material around the metal frames and sew it into place. My mother suffered from chronic asthma and frequently used a spray pump to ease her breathing. My father was considered the boss of the home and business, and my mother followed his lead. Those were the conditions at that time.

I had two sisters: Hannie, the eldest and Lea, who came a year later. Eight years later, I was born and was often referred to as "the latecomer" or, more precisely, "the unexpected one." I surmise from this that I was not planned. I was nicknamed Monkey, because I had big ears that stood out from my head.

I knew very little about my eldest sister, Hannie, because of our age difference. When we were older, she met a man named Ies van Been and his little boy, Appie. Ies worked as a master tailor out of their home next door to ours. There was a rumor that his wife had turned to prostitution and he got a divorce. My sister and he fell in love and got married. Both my parents were enraged at the idea that their daughter was involved with a divorced man, so they did not attend their wedding. Later, things resolved themselves when their first child, Little Lea, was born. They later had another child named Sylvia, named after Ies' mother.

My youngest sister, Lea, studied the so-called Gypsy-style violin at an early age and left home at 18 to join an orchestra that specialized in czardas music. She became independent and traveled all over the country and other parts of Europe.

My mother had four brothers, Louis, Barrent, Hartog and Judas, and two sisters, Keetje and Mietje. My mother's father, Elias Berkelouw, operated a pawnshop, and her brothers Hartog and Barrent, both worked for their father. Later they opened their own jewelry store. Hartog's son, Big Harry, also ended up as a member of the diamond exchange in Amsterdam.

My favorite was Uncle Barrent, who we fondly called Uncle Bear (pronounced and spelled "Beer" in Dutch) because of his big build and athletic physique. He used to do a handstand on one hand for me when we visited him at his store. He was a famous strongman known for being able to rip a telephone book in half.

My uncle Louis was tall and slender but strong as a bull. I was told that he'd been the terror of his neighborhood when he was in his teens. Later, he became a professional card player and gambler and showed me amazing tricks with cards and slight-of-hand tricks with coins.

I called my father Pappa. He was a quiet person and a strong disciplinarian who was probably beaten by his stepfather. He often used a very strong hand on me when I didn't behave according to his liking. At the table, when I didn't want to eat something or if I did anything that he didn't like or permit, he would impatiently tap his fingers on the table as a warning sign. I was always ordered out of the room when business matters were discussed.

I had every material thing I wanted as a child, with plenty of toys and later my own room, a racing bike, fancy scooter, tailored clothes, a soccer club membership, swimming lessons, boxing lessons, dance lessons, pocket money, a portable record player with plenty of records, and outings to the beach in the summer. The many sports I participated in developed my arms and legs. My father would sometimes give a meaningful wink to my mother when he noticed my physique when he thought my back was turned.

Our housekeeper's name was Sienne Niedieck. She was also my nanny, and when her chores were done at night she returned to her home. I would often cry and scream if she didn't take me with her. I lived with her and her family for what felt like weeks and months and my parents did not object. I was very happy to be with her family, despite the fact that they were poor and with no luxuries. They had no electricity, running water, indoor toilet, or heat, yet I felt safe and cozy. I have many fond memories of that part of my life with Sienne.

I had psychological problems and was difficult to deal with when I was a child. Up to about the age of six or seven, or even later, I was an extremely finicky eater. I hated soup, snow peas and a host of other foods. I cried my eyes out when they were placed in front of me at the table. Worst of all, I couldn't stand the taste or sight of milk. If I ate eggs, chocolate, or strawberries, I broke out in hives all over my body. When eating bread, I would take a small piece and roll it between my thumb and forefinger into a tiny ball, then keep it in my mouth and suck on it. I would sit like this for what felt like hours in a dreamlike state.

I went to school and hassled my parents like any young teenager. I wasn't really aware of our Jewish identity because our family wasn't very religious. I do remember that Friday nights were special. There were matzahs for Passover, and a man they called the Chevra used to come to our door and my parents gave me money to give to him that was collected for Jewish burial.

Being Jewish never seemed to be an issue, although I do remember the insult "dirty Jew" getting slung around a number of times. Interestingly, the incident I remember most was when I was sent to a Jewish religious school to prepare for a bar mitzvah. The kid who insulted me was Jewish himself, but it led to a fight anyway. A teacher intervened and when he tried to pull us apart, I grabbed his beard and yanked it hard.

Unsurprisingly, I was kicked out of that school and instead of feeling regret or shame, I felt relieved. It had robbed me of my Sundays, when the soccer club I belonged to had started inviting me to play with the seniors, which was quite an honor. I also hated the hour-long walk to reach the school, where I was obliged to listen to endless religious stories, which I did not believe and made fun of constantly. I was a disturbance and a nuisance in class, and they were glad to get rid of me. The feeling was mutual.

As my parents were busy running their business and my two sisters, being much older than I was, lived their own lives, I somehow felt isolated from my family. It was not that we didn't love one another, but I had the feeling that I was an outsider and didn't belong.

CHAPTER 2

Growing up with Little Harry

I HAD TWO first cousins named Harry. Harry Berkelouw, who was much older than I was, we called Big Harry. Because of our age difference, we didn't interact often. Harry van Rhijn, or Little Harry as we called him, was about a year younger than I was and the two of us were inseparable.

Little Harry's father, David van Rhijn, had two brothers. Uncle Emanuel, a very successful businessman who lived in Brussels, and Uncle Meier, who had been living in America for a long time. Little Harry and I did not attend the same school and during the week we didn't see much of each other. That was left for the weekends, which we usually spent together in his home, where I slept over.

I was certainly not lacking in fun activities. In the summertime, Harry and I had season passes to the Wilgenplas. It was members-only, outdoor recreational park outside the city with a large swimming pool and fancy restaurant. There was also a restricted exercise area that had all kinds of equipment to work out, including several wheels where a person could strap themselves in with both hands and feet and roll around.

We were there practically every vacation day swimming, running, and having fun with friends. Sometimes Big Harry would come. He was very handsome and always had a pretty girl with him. He wore fancy clothing, had manicured hands and worked in his father's jewelry store. He had money to spend and usually ate his lunches at the park's restaurant. Big Harry was an role model for us. Little Harry and I would study him from a distance, following how he handled his fork and knife and how he held his glass when he drank.

Even though I was much younger than Big Harry, I also had a girlfriend – sort of. Her name was Mientje Risse. She was cute, had a turned-up nose and lived on the same street as Little Harry, in a house with a small garden in front. While biking by, I'd wave to Mientje and pretended I would take her out some day, like Big Harry did with his girlfriend. Occasionally I stopped at her garden when I saw her there. I never even held her hand, the only way we touched was like most young teens who have difficulty expressing their desire – pushing, shoving, and pretend-fighting. One day, full of enthusiasm, I rode my bike all the way to her school. It was a long ride and when I arrived, she was nowhere to be found.

Getting to Little Harry's house was also a real journey – 45 minutes on my bike. When school was out on Saturday afternoons, I would spend weekends there. Turning onto his street, I would let out an ear-splitting scream like a war cry. Upon hearing my screech, Harry would promptly run to his balcony and return a warble to me. The signal was also meant to announce my arrival to Mientje.

After dinner, Harry and I listened to our favorite radio programs. Then we played chess until it was time to go to bed. We usually talked deep into the night. Whatever Harry had or did, I had to have or do also, and vice versa. When he joined a soccer club, I joined the same one shortly after. When I joined the boxing club, Little Harry promptly followed. I cannot remember who joined the swim club first but every Wednesday afternoon, which was our half-day off from school, we went swimming in the public indoor pool.

Part of our friendship was friendly competition. We were both athletic and muscular, and we showed off our muscles to each other, bragging. My competition with Harry had its problems, like our transition from knickerbockers to regular long pants. In our early teens, boys wore knickerbockers, or knickers for short. They were longer than the shorts we wore in summer, but shorter than long pants because knickers had a band below the knees that held them up. When Harry and I reached the ripe old age of 14, we jealously looked at other boys our age whose parents allowed them to wear long pants. However, our parents resisted, so we resorted to temporary countermeasures. When we were away from home, we loosened the band that held our knickers up, allowing them to drop to our ankles. The baggy knickers hanging over our shoes became our new style.

Before entering our homes, we hastily returned the band of the knickers to the position our parents expected. However, it didn't take long before most parents caught on to the new style we sported. My own parents, however, were slow to notice that I was one of the sportier types. When they spotted other boys who had dropped their knickers, they were horrified.

"Look at them. How badly they dress. How could their parents allow this?" my mother said.

"At least we're glad that you don't do this, Shjakie," my father added, the last being how my name was pronounced in Dutch.

Harry's parents were a bit more tolerant, and eventually bought him a pair of long trousers, which he proudly showed off to me. How I envied him! I became obsessed and one day I purposely kept my knickers around my ankles when I returned from school. This caused a tumult beyond description. My parents wondered how I could commit this heinous act, saying it looked horrible and cheap. They told me that I shouldn't be coarse like the other boys and to "Hitch up your knickers immediately." I started my counterattack.

"Sure, I'll change my pants. But Aunt Keetje and Uncle David bought long trousers for Harry, so why can't I have a pair?" It took a whole week of nagging and cajoling before my parents capitulated. I talked them into buying me a pair of long trousers at the same department store where Harry's parents had bought his. I also found a kind of polo shirt that looked very American to me. I will never forget the amazing feeling I had when Little Harry and I stood in front of a mirror, admiring our new outfits. We felt ten feet tall.

Of course, now that we were men we had to act like it. Number one on our agenda was cigarettes. All men smoked, so we had to do this as well. The first drag I took made me sick and dizzy. I noticed that Harry's face also turned pale, but we both acted as though we thoroughly enjoyed that first smoke. We proudly looked at each other. Long trousers and a cigarette between our lips. We had arrived. We kept puffing away in those first weeks, courageously fighting nausea and dizziness. These symptoms eventually disappeared and we were deliriously happy.

Harry and I were enthusiastic members of our soccer club, Xerxes. We joined it when we were about ten, in what today would be called the peewees. We gradually moved up the ranks as we grew older and improved our skills and strength. By the time I turned 15, few players were able to match my speed. I played left wing. As soon as I received the ball, I ran. The defenders would see me storming towards them and were unable to block or take the ball away from me. Even though many of them were tougher than I was, my speed and power toppled them on impact, and I kept control of the ball.

The trainers paid special attention to teaching me to use my exceptional speed and strength, but nothing else. It was for that reason I never fully understood the strategy of the soccer game. I relied on speed alone. Little Harry understood the game better. He had a keen sense of strategy and positioning was his strength. He prepared the attacks, deciding which wing to use, or how best to position the two rear-backers on defense. Harry had the potential to become a world-famous professional soccer star like our teammate Faas Wilkes later did, but fate had other plans.

On Sundays, Little Harry and I had our ritual of going to the movies. The Asta Theatre catered to young folks, showing wild-west and space-adventure movies. Tom Mix, a film actor who appeared in almost 300 westerns, and Flash Gordon, the space adventurer played by Buster Crabbe, were our heroes.

Our fantasies about all things American hit a high point the summer when I was 14. It was 1938 and we had great news: Uncle Emanuel van Rhijn announced that he had invited his nephew to visit. The family in America was sending their 19-year-old son, with the wonderfully American name of Babe, to see his uncles and cousins in Europe. He would first stay with Uncle Emanuel in Brussels, who would then drive him to Holland to stay with Little Harry and his family. We could no longer sleep after learning that a "real American" would be visiting us.

We talked till the early morning hours about America and anything that had anything to do with America. Little Harry was one up on me.

"Babe is just as American as Tom Mix and all the other cowboys," he bragged, and then trumped that with "and he's my cousin, not yours."

Sadly, I had to agree with him. Although we were first cousins, Babe was related through his father's side, while we were related through my mother's side. On the day Babe arrived, I was to stay over at Harry's. It was our summer vacation, so there was no school to keep us apart. Harry and I stood on the balcony and waited for what felt like hours. At last, Uncle Emanuel's convertible, top down, stopped in front of the house, and out stepped a lanky young man in khaki sport pants. Harry and I started pushing and shoving each other in excitement. I felt my hands trembling and had trouble breathing, almost choking with joy. Babe waved at us and we almost fainted. Harry remarked how American he looked and I pointed out his loose-fitting shirt with an open collar.

Babe put his luggage (a decidedly American-looking suitcase) down in the living room, and the whole family attacked him with hugs and kisses. When that finished, Harry introduced me as his cousin Jack. I finally got my turn to speak with Babe. Well – sort of. Babe spoke no Dutch at all. The little he knew came out of his mouth with a very heavy American twang. I was now standing in front of Babe, who hovered over me like a tower and the sounds coming out of his mouth were incomprehensible.

"*Whered eerrthar rathy.*" He said in apparent gibberish. I was so anxious that I could no longer speak. "*Whawr thawt thaere huh?*" I heard again, not understanding anything and practically losing my balance out of nervousness.

The next few days were filled with awe and admiration for Babe, who taught us the words "Yes," "No" and "Okay." I was quite a shy boy at the time and had trouble coming close to Babe. I wanted to touch him, just on the sleeve, but could not find the courage. At night, while Harry and I were in bed, we marveled at the way he combed his hair, tied his shoes and buttoned his shirt. There was no end to our fascination, and we began to imitate him, wanting to be like this exotic ideal of Americans.

CHAPTER 3

Homeless — May 10, 1940

The Germans broke their repeated promises to respect the neutrality of Holland and invaded my country on May 10, 1940. They sealed their conquest with a wholesale bombing attack on Rotterdam on May 14 at around one o'clock in the afternoon. Our home on the outskirts of the city. We were hiding in the basement and I can still see the fear on my father's face. The bombs were not landing on our house, but all around us. We could hear the whistle of bombs as they fell, the sound piercing through our ears, then we felt the explosions reverberate in our chest as they shook the ground.

The place that had been my home was no more. The center of the city was destroyed by bombs. I was just weeks away from turning 16 and I can still smell the city smoldering, the rubble emitting a foul stench. Piles of broken bricks and stones buried the streets where buildings once stood. The firestorms that developed after the bombing made us homeless and without possessions. Gone were furniture, clothing, family heirlooms, paintings, art, jewelry, photographs, important documents, and souvenirs – everything had turned to ash.

That night my parents and I fled to a wooded area near our home. From there we saw the entire city of Rotterdam engulfed in flames. The fire destroyed the entire inner city, including my father's electronics factory and his seven retail stores. In the distance, we could see the blades of a windmill turning in the winds of the firestorm. We spent the night camped outside in relative safety.

After tramping from place to place, the Red Cross handed us some clothes and some money. They were very helpful and found us a temporary place to stay. It was an empty apartment with no furniture except folding cots and a few blankets. We were quite fortunate, because some 60,000 families were made homeless. People were in distress, having lost everything. Distribution centers were set up so that those who were lucky enough to live on the outskirts of the city and escape the bombardment could donate any necessary items.

The German High Command did not want over-flying British bombers to see any lights from the cities, so they ordered everyone in the country to black out their windows. No light was allowed to escape. Special squads would be patrolling the streets at night to check for violators, who would be appropriately fined and sometimes punished.

People immediately began buying black paper and pasting it across all their windows, making sure that no light could shine out, then covering them with heavy curtains "just to make sure." The Dutch patrols, the auxiliary police, were dressed in civilian clothes marked with white armbands. They were usually lenient when they spotted bits of light trickling through the windows, especially on the sides which were difficult to cover completely. They sometimes rang doorbells telling residents where the light was shining through, or they yelled from the street: "Lights out – watch your lights!"

My sister, Hannie, and her family had also lost everything. So it made good sense for our families to join forces and rent an empty apartment on Walenburgerweg in Rotterdam. My sister Lea was not with us as she was traveling in the countryside with her orchestra. Despite the tragedy of it all, we were one big happy family. Hannie, Ies, Appie and Little Lea all had a great time, and our parents were elated to be together with their children and grandchildren. For us kids, it was like camping out sleeping on mattresses on the floor since we had no furniture.

Ies was a wonderful person. Always jovial, an incurable optimist, and full of jokes. He was an accomplished master tailor who had received his training as a young man from a famous European designer named Gorki.

Gorki's fame transferred to Ies when he opened his first shop, and he soon had a thriving business. It didn't take long for Ies to re-establish himself after the bombing. I don't know how he acquired the necessary equipment and money so quickly, but soon he was making suits and coats for the many clients he still had.

With my father's businesses destroyed, the only job he could get was clearing rubble from the streets. This proved to be a back-breaking job for a man who had never done hard manual labor in his life. I remember how he came home after work, his hands sore and blistered, and his body in pain.

As a young boy I could not know what a job like that would mean to a man like my father. Hands that never lifted anything heavier than a merchandise box or a heavy chair were now picking up broken bricks, shards of glass, twisted metal sometimes still hot from the fire, and finding bodies under the rubble. It must have been devastating. I can only admire his courage now. However, he had to earn money for his family and at the time that was all he could do. He continued this job for a couple of months.

Other than seeing German soldiers everywhere in the streets in their heavy armored trucks, motorcycles, and horse-drawn war equipment, nothing much changed and people in general began to find the Germans were "nice people after all." The soldiers behaved well, were polite and kept to themselves. They bought loads of merchandise no longer available in their homeland from Dutch stores and paid with "our good old Dutch guilders." This turned out to be good business for shopkeepers and for awhile, things seemed not so bad after all.

Army trucks, loaded with soldiers, filled the streets and sometimes blocked local civilian traffic, grinding everything to a halt. At major intersections, traffic signs were erected in German and for the first few weeks of the occupation, machine gun positions were deployed at strategic locations with soldiers lying prone behind their weapons.

The soldiers, young men in their twenties were mostly "on leave" in Holland. They were members of the Luftwaffe, or the German Airforce, with wings on their collars. Soldiers from the Wehrmacht, which was the main German army, were also on furlough, having conquered most of Western Europe. The naive but stubborn Dutch populace slowly began to realize that their country had been conquered and was now occupied by the Germans.

Learning a trade

Since my high school had been destroyed in the bombardment, my mother suggested that it might be a good idea for me to learn a trade. I was not too enthusiastic about it, but when I heard that my brother-in-law, Ies would take me on as a trainee, I felt better. I liked him a lot and it was always fun to be with him.

Thus began my training in tailoring. The first thing I learned was how to hold and maneuver the fine needle that tailors use, which they push through the material with a needle-ring on their middle finger. Then I learned to make an open loop, which is difficult for a beginner, because the sharp point of the needle usually ends up sticking into your thumb when it comes back up from the material. The next thing I learned was the configuration of the different stitches, locked loops and basting, followed by the correct way to sew a button onto the material. I had advanced to form-stitching the collars of jackets when my father announced that he had found a job for me as an apprentice in the fur business. One of his clients, a woman who operated a fur salon, needed help and would also train me to become a furrier and pay me a salary.

Mrs. Van Merkel was a tall woman with a hoarse voice and reddish-dyed hair. She had a big mouth that housed yellowed teeth surrounded by carelessly painted red lips. First thing in the morning on my first day, she gave me a vacuum cleaner and told me to clean the whole store. In the back of the store was a kitchen. It was quite modern for its time as it was equipped with a range with electric elements.

There was a workshop in the basement where three furriers were at work. My training on the sewing machines started on my second day, and I found the work very difficult. I had to manipulate two serrated rings that turned and acted like clamps to hold two pieces of fur together. In between and slightly above, I had to keep track of a needle that moved up and down forming loops horizontally to sew the two pieces of fur together. I found that if I moved the fur too far up or down, the needle would bend and break. I broke many needles and never really got the hang of running those machines.

Working on the large tables to stretch out the furs and nail them in position was an easier task. The furs were moistened and placed on the table with the skin up. One nail held each piece in place. Long-nose pliers, which also served as a hammer, stretched the skin out in one direction and a second nail was inserted to hold them in the right position. This was repeated along the edge of the fur until the entire piece had doubled in size. When dry, the fur held its new shape. Then I learned how to cut the skin with a specially designed curved knife that had to be honed very often. I liked that work and became quite good at it.

After a few months of doing this kind of work, for which Mrs. Van Merkel paid me a meager salary, my father told me that he had a better job for me that paid double what I was earning. No wonder – he needed me for his own fur business. They had me stretching and cutting rabbit skins that would be made into fur gloves for women. He paid me a handsome salary, and I enjoyed my status as a person who was doing important work. Dad had five or six women working for him who sewed the skins that I had cut out from a cardboard pattern.

Now I understood why my father had sent me to Mrs. Van Merkel. What he really wanted was for me to get some good training. I found out that he had paid her the money for the meager salary that she paid me. My father and Ies had formed a new business. They called it the BeBo Company, a combination of the first two letters of their family names, Been and Boeki. I have no idea how this came about but all of a sudden they both were in the fur business.

The Beginning of my Holocaust

It was now the early fall of 1940, and being sixteen, I was eager to meet some girls to dance with. Little Harry, two friends of ours, one of whom was an amateur boxer, and I found a popular dance hall on the outskirts of the city. It was Saturday night and the place was packed with people. Waiters were busy filling orders and everybody was in a happy mood, laughing in this festive atmosphere.

It was a round building surrounded by a small lake, where people could rent canoes or small rowboats for a relaxing weekend. Inside, tables surrounded by upholstered cozy chairs were arranged in a large circle that hugged the walls, which featured large scenic windows overlooking the lake, leaving the center open for the dance floor.

The floor was something of a novelty. From a distance it looked like a huge chessboard, where each individual square was a colored transparent block that emitted alternating colored lights from within. When the house lights dimmed, and the small orchestra started to play, the colored lights from the floor made a romantic atmosphere for the dancers.

It was a peaceful ambiance where young people laughed and danced and the music was soft and dreamy. We had ordered beer, bottles of which stood in front of us on our table. The lights were not dimmed yet and the orchestra was tuning their instruments. Most of the people around us were Dutch civilians, but here and there we could see German uniforms. "So what," we said, "They seem to be nice people and like to dance just like us. They don't bother us and we won't bother them." Then, out of nowhere –

"*Jude, Jude!*" A shrill voice started screaming: "*Jude, Jude!*" It was shouting the word "Jew" repeatedly. Suddenly there was a deadly silence in the dance hall. Everybody stopped speaking, and within a split second a void opened that swallowed all sound. Blood drained from my head when I saw a tall man in civilian clothes running towards our table, pointing his finger at me screaming in German.

"Are you a Jew?" I felt as if someone was sticking a knife into my stomach. I knew by instinct what his words meant, but I had only learned basic German in school. My mouth was dry and unable to utter a word. I nodded my head, confirming that I was a Jew. The words "*Jude, raus! Raus!*" came out of his distorted mouth. His body stooped over the table, his hatred spewing spittle from his mouth onto my face.

Fear paralyzed me. I was young, very shy and unable to understand what was happening. I got up from my chair like a robot and headed for the exit. I have no recollection of how the four of us left that place. I do remember that my friend Levy, the boxer, threw threatening looks at the German Nazi, but we left terror-stricken on wobbly legs to our homes. A strange kind of hatred had reared its ugly head and blew its foul breath into my face.

When my father heard what had happened, he telephoned the dance hall the next day and spoke to the manager. He assured my father that "the Germans had no right to do this," and he would see to it that "this will not happen again."

CHAPTER 4

First Love Under Occupation

IT WAS NOW later in the fall of 1940. Life had to go on. And go on it did. We moved from temporary housing where our two families were cramped together into a two-level rental apartment my parents found on Schieweg, a major street in Rotterdam. The apartment was nicely furnished with spectacular Gothic furniture with elaborate carvings. It was a self-contained unit in a large brownstone building where the sleeping quarters were on the second floor – my bedroom overlooked the street.

Access from the street required quite some effort; first climbing 15 concrete steps to reach the main entrance hall, which had five doors leading to different apartments, then a very steep staircase that curved at least 25 stairs straight up. That led to a small landing, which after an additional seven steps, finally reached the hallway of the apartment. This was especially difficult for my mother because of her asthma, but she did not complain. During wartime, it was very difficult to get her special asthma medication delivered from Switzerland.

Because we had a home again, things felt like they were returning to normalcy. It wasn't our old home, but it was a place to live. Pappa knew a family who lived around the corner from us. David de Jong was, like my dad, a merchant who owned several retail stores. I met David's son Bram, who was a musician. We became friends almost instantly, and from him I learned much about music, especially the jazz greats such as Django Reinhardt, Hot Club De France, Art Tatum, Glenn

Miller, Count Basie, Benny Goodman, Red Norvo, Lionel Hampton, Louis Armstrong and others. I went to his place often and he would also lend me records so that I could play them at home.

Bram had a sister named Esther, a cute blonde with blue eyes, slightly curly hair and a round baby face. She was an accomplished pianist, having studied the classics practically all her life, and she practiced on her baby grand piano daily in her studio. I never saw much of her because she was usually out with her boyfriend, Piet. He was a talented artist creating beautiful pencil drawings of praying hands and faces. I never paid much attention to Esther. Even though I was nearing the age of becoming interested in girls, I was too busy listening to jazz records with Bram, and besides, she had a boyfriend.

Just as things were starting to feel normal again, official restrictions against Jews came suddenly and in rapid succession. First, the "Proclamations" were pasted on huge billboards erected at strategic locations throughout our city announcing orders and warnings. Radio stations and newspapers were controlled by the Nazis and began blaring propaganda.

On October 17, 1940, the first Proclamation was directed at the entire Dutch population, ordering every citizen aged 15 and older to report to their local municipal registration offices to obtain a "Personal Identity Document." Everyone had to produce a passport-sized photograph with fingerprint and signature and pay five guilders. Failure to follow these instructions was punishable with up to 10 years' imprisonment. This was signed by order of the General of the Armies in the Occupied Territory of the Netherlands. The entire Dutch population was issued personal IDs. The second Proclamation warned that IDs were to be carried at all times by all persons 15 years and older, and had to be produced upon demand by the authorities. Anyone found not carrying their ID would be arrested and punished appropriately. People would say "well, after all, we've been invaded and you have to carry your picture on you at all times ... that isn't so bad."

As there was no school, I was in Bram's studio almost every day. One day, Bram's father suggested that I give Esther French lessons. I don't remember whether he was going to pay me for them, but I agreed. I was not fluent in French, but had a fair working knowledge of the language, having studied it in school for almost three years. I agreed to give her lessons once a week. Up to that point, I had not spoken much to her, other than to say hello or goodbye. I was 16 years old and she was either my age or a couple of years older. I was naturally shy and had no experience with the opposite sex. I was very impressed with her talent and ability to play piano at a concert level.

We sat in her music room together and I taught her the basics of French grammar, which somewhat reduced my shyness, and I became more open. The first few lessons went well. After a few more lessons, I found out that Esther's father had been arrested by the Dutch Nazi police. The next time I came to visit, Bram, Esther, their mother and I were picked up, searched, interrogated and then released after several hours. About a week later, we found out that her father had been arrested for what they claimed was "dealing in foreign currencies," which was against the law during the German occupation. There was no way for his family to visit him or even find out where he was. We were all distraught.

Soon after, during a French lesson, Esther suddenly grabbed my hand. Shy as I was, I didn't know what to do or say. My heart was racing. I knew that she had a boyfriend and the whole thing confused and embarrassed me. But from that moment on the forces of nature took over, slowly in the beginning and more rapidly thereafter. This was the beginning of our love affair, and it grew quite intense. Our relationship caused a bit of trouble with her former boyfriend, who started writing her reams of love letters in beautiful handwriting. She showed me all his letters and never answered them.

I listened to her play for hours. Her interpretations of the works of Mozart, Chopin, Bach, and other masters such as Brahms, Debussy, Franck and Beethoven were beautiful. She flawlessly played them all on her baby grand. This is the first time I was really exposed to this kind of live music. I was very attracted to her and to the music, and I learned so much about the classics. It felt so peaceful, moving and joyous to be surrounded by her music, just the two of us in her studio.

Esther's house was a great place to be because they often held music recitals where many musicians came to play cellos and violins, and my love of classical music increased. We had so much fun together and we went to the movies, even though it had been declared that Jews were not allowed to go. Whether or not our French lessons continued, I can't remember.

Out of nowhere on January 10, 1941, a Proclamation was broadcast on the radio and pasted on special billboards in the streets. Newspapers also carried it in bold print on the front pages: Regulation VO 6/1941. "All Jewish people with at least one Jewish grandparent must register with the population registry." This message was printed in German and Dutch, and unlike previous announcements, which were signed by army commanders, this one was signed by Rauter, the Waffen-SS commander in charge of the dreaded SD – the *Sicherheitsdienst*, an arm of the Gestapo. Failure to comply meant imprisonment or worse.

It seemed like all of the Dutch Jews went to the registration offices at the same time. When we arrived, we had to stand in line for hours. Everyone's major concern was to be on time, before the four weeks we had to comply to the orders were over. From early morning to late in the afternoon, hundreds of families converged upon the building that housed the administration offices, which stayed open beyond their regular closing time trying to accommodate the thousands of people. The waiting lines were exacerbated because entrance to the main office could only be accessed through one door. People were shoving, pushing and yelling when they finally neared that door, only to realize that only one or two persons could pass through. When we finally reached the main office and faced the administrator behind his glass wicket, we were asked to produce our personal ID card. He checked our names off a list to register us.

In February 1941, two events happened in rapid succession. In Amsterdam, where the majority of Dutch Jews lived, entire districts were suddenly blocked off. Anyone who looked Jewish or was thought to be Jewish was picked off the streets and loaded on open trolleys and carried away, leaving no means of finding them. Homes were ransacked and men, women and children were dragged out onto the street, beaten and sometimes killed. The perpetrators of this unspeakable barbarity were not the "nice soldiers" we saw in streets, but the dreaded *Grüne Polizei*, the para-military arm of the SS that had been hidden from view, clouded in secrecy. Many of them looked fierce, the backs of their thick necks protruding from under their frightful steel helmets. They wore ankle length green coats with black jackboots sticking out from underneath.

News of this event spread like wildfire throughout Holland. People who witnessed it could not believe their eyes. Some courageous young non-Jewish men tried to stop the Germans and drag the Jews away or pull them from the trolleys. They were hopelessly outnumbered and mercilessly beaten by three or four bullies, who threw them into the lorries with the Jews and carried them away. They also were never seen again.

Incredibly, the entire Dutch population rose up against this atrocity. They vehemently protested "the treatment of our Dutch Jewish brethren" and demanded the prompt return of all those who had been carried off. Several bishops openly spoke out against this "ruthless action against innocents" and many churches conducted prayer services. It was more than amazing that a small country like Holland challenged the then-mighty Germans.

When the Germans ignored these protests, the entire nation went on strike. Trade unions advised their members to strike. Anything that could move – trains, streetcars, taxis – stopped operating. Public buildings and municipal offices shut their doors. Workers, administrators, postmen, tradesmen all went on "sick call." Still, the Germans did not make a move, but it was a menacing silence that filled the air and everyone held their breath.

As was feared by all, they retaliated. Their Proclamation was repeated every half-hour on the radio and plastered on billboards throughout the streets:

> *15 criminal insurgents have been taken into custody and shot to death as a result of subversive activities against the German State. 50 hostages from the former Dutch Army's Officers Corps have been taken into custody. Unless all workers throughout the Occupied Territory of the Netherlands return to their respective workplaces immediately, 25 hostages will be shot without any further notice.*

The order was signed by Hanns Albin Rauter, Higher SS- and Police-Leader and General Commissioner of Security of the Waffen-SS. The impact of this blackmail and murder forced everyone to return to work, thus ending the strike. Some resistance against the German occupiers continued, but it was futile and the retribution was always deadly. With every move against them, the Germans murdered more hostages; even non-Jews were randomly picked up from the street and kept as hostages against any future resistance.

Further impossible conditions were imposed. Jews were not allowed to attend schools, colleges or universities, and Jewish teachers lost their jobs. Doctors, dentists, nurses and medical professionals were forbidden to work in clinics or hospitals. Slowly and steadily, there were more and more things that we, as Jews, could no longer do. We were no longer allowed to have radios leaving us cut off from the world. Then, we could no longer go to the pool, the beach or libraries.

On September 15, 1941, everywhere, against the wishes of the Dutch people, signs were erected: "FORBIDDEN FOR JEWS." These signs could be found on all restaurants, cafes, markets, parks, movie theaters, hotels and museums. The last straw, for me, was the directive that Jews had to be in their homes with a curfew from 8 p.m. to 6 a.m. each day of the week. It felt like a death sentence. I now fully realized that we were occupied by hatred and evil.

Just like other Jews, my father and all our relatives eventually lost their jobs. All Jewish businesses were taken over by so-called "administrators" and owners were unceremoniously thrown out and made to transfer all their assets to a bank that the Germans had set up for this purpose.

The unbelievable had happened. Raids and shootings in the streets had changed everything. I told my father, "If the Germans come for me, they're going to have to kill me or I'm going to kill them." I felt like I could never let them catch me, otherwise it would be game over.

"Son, you've seen too many Hollywood movies." was his response, he thought I was being overly dramatic. I meant what I said – I was willing to fight to the death.

PART II

FUGITIVE ON THE RUN AND A NEW LIFE IN FRANCE

CHAPTER 5

Into Hiding and on the Run

IT WAS ALMOST one year later, in 1942, that we had to return to update our ID cards. The administrator checked our names off a list and then stamped a bold black "J" across our ID. Amongst friends and relatives, jokes were rampant. "As if now that we have this official J, we can be sure we're not Catholic," they said and laughed. Because Esther's mother was Christian, it made Esther "half Jewish" under the existing Nazi rules, which meant she didn't have to have this special J.

Many Jews went into hiding. Later, young non-Jews who wanted to avoid forced labor in Germany, went into hiding as well. Personal IDs were being falsified, entire documents were created with a new name and without the dreaded J. It was very difficult to imitate the official documents, and some fake IDs were better than others.

I was now jobless and our situation looked increasingly hopeless. The Germans started picking up boys to work in Germany, or so we heard. On May 3, 1942, they also instituted a decree that all Jews must wear a yellow Star of David, visible on their clothing while in public. They even charged us four cents for each star.

For two days I was walking proudly in the street with the star on my clothing, chest sticking out and head held high, wanting to show those Nazis we were proud Jews and not afraid. But events were getting increasingly more dangerous. I was rebellious and decided to stop wearing the star and started searching for a false ID. I often slept over at Esther's house because I felt safer there than in my own home. I would stay on the top floor with Bram but would sneak out after everyone was asleep and go downstairs to her room, which was on the same floor as her parents' bedroom.

My parents became increasingly concerned about our family's safety and decided to send my younger sister, Lea, and me into hiding in a city in the southern part of Holland named 's-Hertogenbosch, or Bois-Le-Duc in French. My sister had a friend she had known for a long time whose family was considered extremely anti-German, trustworthy and more than happy to hide us in their big home. We celebrated Lea's birthday on September 4, 1942. After hiding in their house for about three months, we got a warning that a raid was imminent. I ran out of the house and tried to hide in the street.

I was alone in a strange neighborhood. I was a shy 17-year-old teenager, used to obeying my parents. I had never made any major decisions on my own. There I was, without valid identity papers, everything in defiance of the laws that the Nazis had imposed. I knew that if they caught me, something terrible would happen. Danger lurked everywhere. I feared not only German soldiers, but Dutch collaborators as well.

I lived as a fugitive. It was autumn, heading into winter. During the day, I tried to lie low in some hiding place. I moved stealthily at night, hoping to find a better hiding place for the next day. No one challenged me, but hunger, terror and fear were my constant companions, along with pigs and cows, as I often spent the night in stables. I appreciated the warmth of their bodies, since by now it was the beginning of Octobe and the weather was getting cold.

I was lucky to be in the south of Holland, where people were predominantly Catholic and stubbornly opposed to the German occupiers. Eventually, I approached some of them, and I owe my life to the folks who helped me. They let me sleep in barns, stables, and sometimes even their homes. They fed me and gave me warm clothes. Still, every night I had to search out a new place to hide. I did not have a plan; fear drove me from place to place. I never knew where I would end up. Finally, I decided to go back to Rotterdam, where at least I knew my way around and knew some people who might be able to help me.

Of course, getting to Rotterdam required a train ticket and a fake ID because Jews were no longer allowed to travel on public transportation. I had neither and no money. I knew that danger lurked all around me. Still, I decided to take the risk and sneak into the railroad station. The station was dark like the houses because of the wartime blackout. That helped me sneak in without a ticket and while my heart was pounding, I found the platform with the destination sign "Rotterdam."

I jumped into a train compartment with just a few travelers and found a seat. My luck held out. No conductor showed up to check for tickets, and I arrived in Rotterdam without incident. Once there I remembered that my non-Jewish friend, Joan van Krieken, lived near the station. She had been a fan of the soccer club I had played for. She was a cute girl that everyone liked, and I thought that she would probably be able to help me.

Even though it was late at night, she and her parents received me with open arms. Her father, a lanky, tall man with graying hair, and her mother (a woman born in America who spoke flawless Dutch) would not hear my protestations and insisted I stay overnight. She cooked delicious food and reminisced about her youth in the United States. I stayed with these kind people for about a week. They treated me well and made me feel at home.

Joan's father was active in his opposition to the Germans and managed to get me a phony ID. It was only a fair piece of counterfeit work, but it was better than nothing. All of us kept an open ear for possible danger. I stayed away from the windows and I spoke softly. When visitors came by, I hid in a closet, remembering to empty my bladder beforehand if there was enough time. Once, when a visitor came without warning, I had to spend a whole afternoon in that closet with a painfully full bladder.

I knew that staying too long in one place was dangerous for both me and them. I didn't want to put these courageous people in jeopardy and decided to leave. I left at night when it was dark, hesitant to leave such a cozy place and to plunge headlong into risk and uncertainty once more. They hugged me and wished me good luck. I remember them saying, "These hard times will be over soon, and before you know it, things will be back to normal."

One night, I was staying in an empty air-raid shelter, damp and cold, and spotted a dilapidated trailer home standing deserted in a field near the edge of town. It was mustard-brown, had rust spots all over and rested on two flat tires. One of its tires had sunk into the mud, making it lean to one side. I pried at the rear door and it screeched open. By good fortune there was a pile of dirty blankets on the floor.

I shut the screeching door behind me, crawled into the stack of blankets and fell into a deep sleep. I slept for days almost continuously, letting one day follow the night, occasionally going outside just to relieve myself. I was in a daze, dreamless at night, blasé during the day, probably because I wasn't eating and had no money to buy food. It was cold. Condensation formed on the inside of the trailer; when I woke up, I felt drops of moisture fall on my face. I just dug deeper under the blankets and slept on. I didn't know where my parents and the rest of my family were during this time.

I came out of the daze one morning and I realized I needed to move on. I needed help. I decided to go to Amsterdam and ask my cousin Big Harry for help, who was living there in a beautiful, luxurious apartment. He was not considered Jewish according to the Nazi laws. His non-Jewish mother had sworn to a Nazi court that Harry was not her son by her husband, but from an extramarital affair with a non-Jew. Harry was considered a Christian or, by the Nazis, an "Aryan."

Before undertaking the dangerous train trip to Amsterdam, I went back to Joan's house to shave and clean up. Joan's parents insisted that I stay the night. Before I left the next morning, Joan plucked my thick black eyebrows to make me look less Jewish. Her dad gave me a nice fedora to cover my pitch-black hair. He added a briefcase to make it look like I was on business. I was going to buy a ticket openly, and Joan pressed money into my hands – it was more cash than I needed for even ten tickets!

CHAPTER 6

Escape from My Overcoat

IT WAS BROAD daylight when I arrived at the station and the man behind the counter did not even look at me when I said, "A one-way ticket to Amsterdam, please."

"First or second class?" he asked.

"Second class," I replied. I thought that if there were Germans on the train, they'd ride first class.

I tilted the fedora low over my forehead and ran to the platform where my train to Amsterdam was ready to depart. I had to press through a crowd of ordinary people dressed in street clothes and, to my dismay, lots of uniformed German soldiers. I hurried past them with butterflies in my stomach and boarded the train. I felt different from my fellow passengers, as if I had entered the compartment without any clothes on. Should I take a seat? *Too dangerous*, I thought. Best to stand, look away from people and stare out of the window. Occasionally I turned around and scanned the compartment. I tried to study as many people as I dared. "Eliminating risks," I said to myself.

When the train pulled out of the station, I let out a sigh of relief. That relief turned to panic at the first station stop, where I saw several people in black uniforms board the train. The uniforms identified them as Dutch Nazis, or enemy collaborators. Instinctively, I moved from my spot at the window and ducked into a toilet. I stayed there, not daring to come out until the train reached Amsterdam.

When I got off the train, I fully realized the danger I was in. There I was, a Jewish teenager with strong Semitic features walking into a busy square without the obligatory yellow Star of David, carrying a clearly falsified ID. Hat deep over my head, collar of my brown overcoat turned up, I crossed the large square until I reached the stop where all Amsterdam streetcars pick up passengers. I found the stop for the car that would take me to my cousin's home and boarded as soon as the doors opened.

As I rode I began to focus on the sunny, crisp day in early November. There wasn't a cloud in the sky. I was wearing my made-to-measure overcoat, tailored by my brother-in-law. It was stylish, with a knee-length cut and sizable shoulder pads that were in vogue at the time. It kept me warm and comfortable. As I stood in a corner of the car, I realized that for a moment I was witnessing a sense of normalcy with the everyday scurrying of people getting on and off the car and felt somewhat relieved.

Then, after about five minutes, I sensed someone staring at me. I turned to look. It was a young man not taller than I, wearing a short leather jacket, who continued to stare intensely at me. I stared right back.

Then he approached me and commanded, "Give me your ID."

What a police state Holland had become! Without any reason, Nazi sympathizers could assail you. I wasn't scared and felt ready to deal with him.

"Oh sure," I said with a sigh. "ID again? Do you know how many times this happens to me in a day? I'm Italian and people seem to think I look like a Jew. I am getting tired of this."

Once I handed it to him, he studied the phony ID that Esther had helped me get. He seemed unsatisfied. My ID was clearly fake; it didn't take a genius to see that.

"Come with me," he barked. "We'll figure out what to do with you at headquarters."

He motioned for me to get off at the next stop and he was right behind me. He pushed me out of the streetcar onto the street. I had no idea where I was or where he was taking me, but the word "headquarters" sounded frightening.

We walked for about five minutes and passed a tall individual in a black uniform; they greeted each other with the "Heil Hitler!" salute. Now the adrenaline in my body kicked in. I felt danger crawling towards me. Once we rounded a corner, my inner voice said, "It's now or never, Jack. No good awaits you at headquarters. Get away from this guy now!"

I had developed a strong sense for danger and felt it throughout my body. He was walking on my left side and I on his right. I surveyed the wide avenue that was divided by a median encircled with short bushes. My body, not my brain, took command.

My body stiffened and launched me into a run. But he sensed it at once. His right hand shot out and seized the heavily padded left shoulder of my overcoat, his fingers clutching like the talons of a hungry eagle.

Then two things happened within a split second. First, in the ensuing struggle, the flat briefcase that I carried in my left hand somehow got caught between my legs, forcing me to lose my balance. I fell face down onto the pavement. To protect my face, I spread my arms out in front of me. When I hit the ground, my face landed on my forearms, softened by the sleeves of my overcoat.

Still gripping my shoulder-pad, my assailant to lose his balance as well and fell on top of me. The sudden movements and the fact that I had both arms spread outwards while falling caused my overcoat to open, and I felt both shoulder pads began to slide off me as I crawled forward, terrified. I wanted to get rid of that beast on my back and as I moved forward, I felt the entire coat sliding off my body.

Holding a practically empty overcoat, he released his grip and went to catch my right foot. Somehow most of the overcoat had moved to the side under his body and when I looked back, I saw his face not far away from my left foot.

Like lightning, my left leg exploded into a frenzy of violent kicks that hit him in the middle of his face. Again and again I kicked at his face, harder and harder, with as much strength as I could muster. My rage spewed out at him – my tormentor, my enemy, this foul cancer crawling behind me like a poisonous snake.

No longer did I feel his hand on my leg. He had let go. I was now free of him. Without thinking, my powerful, soccer-trained legs straightened out and started running, running, running at full speed, away from that evil calamity. Gone were my overcoat, borrowed fedora, briefcase with all its contents and false ID. For a fleeting moment I dared look back at my victim who lay on top of my overcoat with me no longer in it.

I have no recollection of how long I ran, or where I was going. I was strong and in top physical shape, well trained for running at top speed, having played soccer for five years. At one point I heard a noise behind me. I started to run faster, believing that someone was chasing me. Indeed, someone was. He was on a bicycle, yelling, "Well done, well done! Jump on! Jump on my bike!"

What a lucky break – I jumped on the back and the man pedaled like the dickens. There were no tires on his bike rims because of the rubber shortage. It was a bumpy ride because the tires were makeshift pieces of wood. I am still grateful to the man who offered his help, he dropped me off somewhere and I never saw him again.

Somehow, I found the apartment where Big Harry lived. When he opened his door, I fell to the floor exhausted. Only then did he notice the blood on my left shoe. I feared it to be mine but soon understood that the blood belonged to that monster I had kicked. "I must have really injured or even killed him," I said with a shudder. The heel of my shoe had repeatedly hit him right in the middle of his face and that could have broken his nose or his neck. I increasingly felt that he was dead, because he did not follow me and just lay there motionless.

Big Harry nodded in amazement when he heard my story. He thought it wise not to stay at his place, in case I had been followed. He fed me a wonderful meal and gave me some money and a raincoat. I followed his advice and moved on, back to Rotterdam. Life was becoming a hell on earth, each day filled with terror.

CHAPTER 7

The Long Staircase

THE RIDE FROM Amsterdam left me tense; my nerves were shot, and I was wobbly all over. Having no ID, nor star on my clothing and being out in the city streets beyond curfew meant I could be arrested or shot. It was November 1942 and I was still on the run from the Gestapo.

Walking through the rubble – all that remained of the inner city – the piles emitted a foul stench. Broken bricks and stones had buried the streets where buildings once stood. A cramp in my abdomen, a desperate call of nature, brought me back to the present moment. Darkness had set in; the night had become blacker than black and a wind rose, bone-chillingly cold. Where to go? Where to go in heaven's name? Afraid to be discovered in the open, I got out of the inner-city ruins as fast as possible. I thought perhaps I'd be able to hide in some doorway.

I looked desperately for a public restroom without success. After more than an hour, I lost my ability to walk or stand straight under the urgency of my bowels. I finally stooped on somebody's porch, unable to control my bodily functions any longer. I hastily undid my trousers and underwear and unloaded right there. I pity the poor residents who would find a huge dump in front of their entrance the next morning. I also felt ashamed, but there was little I could do about it. I looked around and realized that in my quest for a bathroom I had unconsciously wandered toward the furnished apartment that my parents had rented.

At the time, I had no idea where my parents were. I knew that my father had received an order to report to a "work camp" somewhere in

Holland and that he had gone there to "save the family," as if anything could save us. The whereabouts of my mother, sisters and the rest of our family were also unknown to me. Searching in my clothes, I found that I still had the key to the apartment in my back pocket.

I let myself believe that maybe my mother had returned there. Stealthily, I moved closer, crossing the street with my heart in my throat, hoping that there were no patrols to spot me. Then I climbed the concrete stairway that led to the front door. I carefully stuck my key into the lock and gave a sigh of relief as it opened with click. Then I climbed the many flights of stairs that led from the street to the entrance of the apartment. There was a young married couple sitting in our living room – very surprised to see me.

"Who are you and where is my mother?" I asked. They explained that my parents had rented them the apartment so they could take care of it. They told me that they had not seen my mother, nor heard from her in a while.

"Have you heard from my sister, Lea?"

"No" was their answer, "We haven't seen anyone from your family."

I explained that life was getting more difficult, and they nodded with sympathy. I explained that I just needed to sleep and to spend a night in my own bed again. I went to my room to retire and immediately fell into a deep, dreamless sleep.

I sensed that morning had come, but before I could open my eyes, I felt the pressure of something cold against my temple and heard a metallic clicking sound, followed by the bellowing command, "Get out of bed!"

Now awake and completely disoriented, I stared into the stern face of a man – a Dutch Nazi collaborator. This man, with his long nose and small, graying Hitler moustache, dressed in plainclothes, kept watch over me as he held a small pistol against my head.

"Get up and get dressed," he repeated.

My bed was not far from the window that faced the street. The first thing I did was look out the window to see if there was a police vehicle waiting out front. There was no vehicle or evidence of police backup. My brain was thinking ahead of my body.

Incredibly, I was not scared or nervous. Immediately, I thought that he sought me out because of the trouble I'd encountered in Amsterdam on the streetcar. I got dressed while he and the young wife stood around, not saying much. Finally, she asked if she could give me a sandwich and he said that was okay.

As I accepted the paper bag with the sandwich from the young woman, the traitor stood behind me and the top of the long staircase loomed in front of me. I felt as if the stairs were taunting me to flee down the more than 30 steep steps and away from this peril. A bolt of energy shot through my body, an instinctive urge to run. I threw the sandwich bag into the air as a distraction and then leaped, half falling, half jumping down the stairs, skipping six to seven steps at a time. In a matter of seconds, I landed at the front door.

As I opened it, the fresh air that hit my face gave me additional strength. Outside, I still had another steep flight of concrete steps to descend to get to the street. I cleared the last dozen or more stairs in one risky, huge jump, without touching any of them. I landed on hands and feet at street level. I don't know how I made it out so fast. I could have easily broken my neck with that jump, but I only scraped my hands. They were bloody, but I felt no pain. I regained my balance and sprinted towards the corner of the street as if I were flying. A hundred yards away, I turned the corner, looking behind me. I could see my pursuer following me. He had just reached street level.

I kept running, knowing that I had a hundred yards advantage over him, an older man who certainly could not keep up with my pace. I turned a second corner, and spotted a green steel door that stood ajar, leading to an inner courtyard. I jumped through the door and kicked it shut behind me. The terrace had tall, overgrown hedges setting off the little plots and gardens that belonged to the residents of the surrounding apartment buildings.

I crawled under the lowest branches of a hedge, and they bent back over me, hiding me well. No one followed me, but I could hear police sirens in the street. The police, alerted by the guy who had confronted me, apparently did not realize that there was an entry to this inner garden. They had not noticed the steel door as I had kicked it closed behind me.

Fortunately, some residents of the surrounding apartments became aware of what was happening. From their windows, they saw me hiding in the bushes. On the other side of their building, they could see police searching the area in front of their apartment. The residents fortunately belonged to the "good third" of the Dutch people. These people didn't just watch – they ran back and forth between the two sides of the buildings and, from the balconies that overlooked the terrace, whispered encouragement : "Stay where you are, you're okay there."

They kept protecting me throughout the morning and early afternoon until they saw the police leave. They motioned for me to come out. When I appeared, stiff and cold, they yelled, "Well done ... well done, good for you!"

I owe my life to these people, something I shall never forget.

CHAPTER 8

From Prison to the Red Light District

I EVENTUALLY FOUND myself sitting in my sister Hannie's living room with her and her husband, Ies, and our mother. I don't remember how I got there. Their lives had not yet been disrupted by the Germans. I, on the other hand, was very scared, hungry and cold – so miserable that I needed to be with my family. I hadn't been there long before my visit was cut short by loud knocks at the door. A shock went through my entire body. I sensed they were coming for me; I sensed it without seeing them.

My muscles tensed and I flew from the table. I ran through the kitchen to the rear door and into the small garden at the back, only to see the dark shadow of a man behind the hedge at the far end of the garden. Clearly he was there to head me off. Again, without thinking, I jumped over the hedge, which was about five feet high. As I cleared it, I aimed my body directly at him. He fell backward as I landed on top of him. The impact must have stunned him. Unfortunately, in my landing, I twisted my left foot and I felt a flaming pain when I tried to get up. I tried to ignore the agony as much as I could and started running away. Nonetheless, I put a good distance between myself and danger and forced myself to continue.

That's when I heard gunshots. Whoever fired at me must have been a lousy shot because I never even heard the ping of bullets hitting near me. Fear and terror kept me running as fast as I could, despite the pain and the bullets. Eventually, the pain in my foot nearly paralyzed me.

In the middle of the next avenue, high piles of bricks were stacked up, remnants of the German bombardment of Rotterdam. I could go no further and pulled myself on top of the bricks. I flattened my body as best I could, knowing that this really wasn't a good hiding place. Of course it wasn't. A man saw me and yelled, "He's here!"

Several police dragged me off the bricks onto the street and handcuffed me. Suddenly the man I had escaped on the staircase appeared. He pulled his signature move, once again holding his pistol against my head and said, "We'll shoot to kill if you try to escape again." I thought it was all over for me now. These Dutch traitor policemen could certainly congratulate themselves on catching public enemy number one – the dangerous outlaw, the teenager Jack Isaac Boeki, whose only crime was being a Jew.

Soon a crowd of people gathered, all curious about what was happening. My eyes picked Robert Gillaine out of the crowd. Robert was an official on the board of directors at our soccer club. He held his bike with him, one hand on the saddle. His eyes focused on me. Staring intensely, he guardedly moved his other hand towards his bike. He kept moving his eyes up and then back down to his bike.

I caught the silent signal. He was offering that I take his bike and ride away. I couldn't risk that, not in this situation, so I slightly shook my head while moving my eyes side to side. Many events of the past have disappeared from my memory, but this token of support from a righteous and courageous Christian will always stay with me.

A police car arrived and they shoved me into the back with guards on each side. Not a word was spoken during the ride to the police headquarters. I had no idea what was going to happen to me, but strangely, I felt no fear. They led me to a second-floor office where a gray-haired man was sitting at a desk. A young man in his early twenties removed my handcuffs, ordered me to empty all my pockets and then began to search me.

"You want me to strip-search him?" he asked the older man. The older guy snarled back, "Just remove his necktie and take his ring." He confiscated the small gold ring Esther had given me.

When they found nothing else of interest, they led me to another section of the building. It looked like the inside of a prison – which, in fact, it turned out to be. I remember that it was very brightly lit and that many of the cell doors had a large Star of David attached to them. They opened a cell door shoved me inside. I could hear them attach a Star of David to my door after it was closed. They didn't want to lose sight of the fact that they had caught another Jew.

The inside of my cell was pristinely clean; it looked recently built. Once alone, I examined every nook and cranny for a possible escape but found none. I then exercised – jumping and sparring – in training for a possible escape. I pictured the man who had hunted me down standing in front of me. If I ever had the chance, my aim would be precise and deadly. Punching the air, I said, "I'll kill you with just one blow to the head. Just you wait." I pictured myself blasting my way out of that prison.

They fed me a thin cabbage soup that did not taste bad. At times, they led me to an open courtyard surrounded by high walls where I could walk in the open air for a while with other prisoners.

They kept me in that cell for four days. It felt like I stood still, while time went on around me. One morning, things began to happen. My cell door opened and two young men led me downstairs, where my captor met me on the landing. He handcuffed me and said sternly, "We're sending you to Westerbork and if you try to escape again, we'll shoot you!"

Westerbork was a transit camp in Holland where people were held for deportation. I found myself among a group of about 30 other prisoners, mostly old men, women and some children. They put us into an open shed awaiting transportation. Some prisoners carried suitcases bulging with personal belongings, while others held rolled-up blankets or pillowcases filled with meager belongings. It was obvious they had been allowed little time to pack and had left in great haste.

Four men, rifles slung over their shoulders, appeared and commanded us to follow. Doors opened and I I spotted my mother waiting there. Obviously, she had been informed that I was being "put on transport," as the expression went at that time. Some kind-hearted soul had given her the opportunity to see her son off. We were able to quickly hug and kiss, while I whispered in her ear, "Don't worry, Mamma, I'll get out."

They put us in buses to the train station, where a regular passenger train was waiting for us. The four guards who had taken us from the prison were replaced by four other guards, who were standing by the train. They told us to enter the train and to my great surprise they removed my shackles. This greatly increased my chance of escape. It seemed unlikely that this new crew had been informed about my talents as an escape artist.

As soon as the train started to move, I looked to see how I might get out. Four guards stood in front of each exit, so I could not get out that way. Luckily, I could move around the car freely and my attention focused on the toilet. I checked the handle – it was locked.

"I have to go," I said to one of the guards. He took a key from his pocket and opened the door. Once inside, I found no way to get out of there either.

After a short while the train reached Amsterdam Central Station. We were ordered out of the train and to take all our belongings. I had nothing. The others who were taken from their homes, had at least been able to bring suitcases, bags, trunks and pillowcases stuffed with clothes, which were now deposited on the platform in a neat row. One of the guards cupped his mouth with his hands and yelled, "Jews, listen! You must carry your own baggage!"

The guard saw that there were many who would be unable to carry their own belongings, so he added, "Who will volunteer to help the older people?" I immediately shot forward.

"I'll help," I said, picking up a yellow suitcase. Three other young men also volunteered and four guards posted themselves near us, motioning to follow them.

Our little group proceeded slowly from the train platform to the exit of the railroad station. Parked near one of the side entrances were two buses, their front and rear doors wide open. There did not seem to be any guards near the buses, just the drivers.

I placed the suitcase I was carrying inside the rear of one of the buses and then returned to the platform where the rest of the prisoners were waiting. There were still at least 20 pieces of luggage left to be picked up, so I visualized several trips back and forth to the waiting buses.

The next item I picked up was a white canvas bag that looked like a large laundry bag. The opening on top of the bulging bag was tied loosely with a grayish cord, where a toy popped its head out. I picked up the bag by the top and swung it over my left shoulder.

Suddenly, I was surrounded by people coming from all different directions. Several trains must have arrived at the same time from different platforms, and now poured their passengers out, all rushing in my direction. By good fortune, they surrounded and blocked me from view of the men who guarded me.

I ducked instinctively and turned the bag upside down. All its contents spilled out onto the floor, the white-and-brown wooden toy dog waggled from side to side as it rolled out of sight. People almost stumbled over the stuff on the floor and stopped to help pick things up, creating a jam. I dared look up through the mass of people and saw no guards, so I stayed low and let myself blend in with the crowd.

Head down, I walked out of the station surrounded by hundreds of people. I crossed a small bridge at the far end of the square, and a few blocks away, I found myself in the middle of the notorious Amsterdam Red Light District. Soon I was among prostitutes who were plying their trade in the gathering dusk. They weren't in their windows but walking out on the street.

"Looking for a good time?" one of them asked. I politely declined, but this gave me an idea – I decided to make myself look like a young prostitute, a great cover in case the guards came looking for me. I rolled my pants up to my knees and asked to borrow a scarf from one of the women to cover my head and tied it under my chin. I tightened the belt of my overcoat to display my narrow waist, and in moments, I had transformed from escaped Jewish boy to streetwalking prostitute. I didn't want to stick around for too long to test my disguise; I wanted to get the hell out of there. I risked reentering the station dressed as a girl, avoided the conductor and somehow got on a train back to Rotterdam.

CHAPTER 9

The Birth of Pieter Lutgert

WHEN I ARRIVED safely back in Rotterdam, I went to Nolensstraat where Hannie lived and rapped on the window saying, "I'm okay, I escaped." I'm not even sure if anyone heard me but I had to move on. Life in Holland had become hell. How could I escape? Where could I hide? Who could I trust? I looked up at a bird in the sky – if only I could take wing and fly away. I tried to shake off the desperation, but the bleakness of my prospects and the dead end of my situation did not go away. I had to find a way out.

I sometimes stayed off and on with Esther and Bram, their seamstress, Miss Cor, and in random hiding places they found for me. I must have also gone back to seek refuge at Joan van Krieken's place because I distinctly remember being with her family and taking a huge risk by listening to a BBC radio newscast, even though we were forbidden to even own a radio. We strained to hear the details of how a French General named François Darlan had been assassinated in Algiers. Since it was an English newscast, I didn't understand the word "assassinated," and asked her father what it meant. This put the date as December 24, 1942.

Eventually, I was reunited with my family and thankfully the Dutch underground found hiding places for my parents, my sister Lea and I, in a small city called Ede. We were not together but in three different locations. The people who hosted me were very nice and treated me well. I believe their family name was Willems or Willemsen, but I can't remember when this happened or how long I stayed in their home.

I knew that my parents and sister were hidden in the same city but didn't know their address. The underground allowed the exchange of short letters and notes to make life more livable. To make things more interesting, I made up small crossword puzzles and sent them to my sister. That was how we secretly communicated back and forth.

A man who was part of the underground visited us once every two weeks or so to bring us news. I remember even being allowed to visit my parents in their hiding place. Sometime later I was alerted that a raid was in the making. I immediately left my hiding place but can't remember where I went. I most likely snuck on the train back to Rotterdam and moved between hiding places. I would spend a day in one spot, and a few days in another. It's impossible to remember them all. It became almost impossible to find hiding places because of all the risks involved.

Human smugglers

There were rumors going around that there were people who could get you out of Nazi-occupied Europe. For a hefty price, they would take you from France across the Pyrenees into Spain. Big Harry, who lived in Amsterdam, did a lot of traveling because he was in the diamond trade. He looked me up while he was passing through Rotterdam. How he found me was one of the riddles that always surrounded my thoughts of him. He might have been active in the resistance against the Germans, but I never found out.

Harry and I discussed a scheme to get me to Portugal and he promised to investigate it in detail. He said he would contact my girlfriend Esther, who knew where I was hiding most of the time, and give her the details of what he found out.

The couple who would carry out such an undertaking would take groups of four to Perpignan, located near the border between France and Spain. Collaborators would meet the refugees there and take them to neutral Portugal. Their price was high and included all travel from Holland to the destination. Big Harry gave Esther the address of the couple that I would have to go meet. He said that I should not worry about the money because he would finance the deal. What he found strange – and did not like – was that these people specified that they wanted to interview me alone.

Nonetheless, I agreed to meet them. When I arrived at their place, we shook hands. The man and his wife seemed like a nice couple. They explained that though it had succeeded in the past, the trip was fraught with danger. It would take more than two weeks to reach our destination. Crossing the Pyrenees would be difficult because of German patrols guarding the border. Warm clothing was essential, as well as strong boots for climbing. Food, housing and false papers would be included in the deal.

While they were describing what to do and what not to do, the doorbell rang. Was I ever relieved and surprised when Big Harry walked in. He laughingly said his hellos and when he went to shake my hand, he pressed a small piece of paper into it in such a way that my interviewers didn't notice. He spoke about some financial arrangements and left shortly afterwards.

As soon as I could do so surreptitiously, I read Big Harry's message. It contained just one scribbled word: "Traitors." Somehow, he had found out that this couple was in the employ of the Gestapo. After taking the refugees' money, they would meet them at a safe house, where the Gestapo would promptly have them arrested.

I kept my composure and calmly announced, "I like your plan. I would like to go with your next group. Let me go and quickly get you the money. My uncle said he would lend it to me and I want to pay you promptly, half in advance as you suggested." When I hit the street, I ran as fast as my powerful soccer legs would carry me.

Finding places to hide kept getting more difficult. Then, there was a glimmer of hope, we learned that the Germans were looking for volunteers to build the so-called "Atlantic Wall," a fortification along the North Sea coast, running from Norway to Spain. This was to defend against an Allied invasion, which they feared would eventually come.

The idea of joining these volunteers intrigued me, even though there was no guarantee it was a safe move. Dutchmen did the hiring for these jobs, but that still left open all kinds of questions. What kind of people would they be? Could they be trusted any more than the couple who had promised safe passage to Portugal? Could I tell them that I was a Jew? Would I be better off not telling them anything and just applying for the job using my false ID?

Esther decided to do some scouting for me. She found out that it wasn't difficult to get accepted. There were only two requirements, applicants had to be at least 20 years old and have a valid ID card. The Germans didn't care about anything else. They needed bodies able to do the work – the more the better. Tall, short, thin or fat did not matter.

Work would mainly consist of pouring cement and light carpentry. The work would be paid. Meals would be provided, as well as housing in large barracks. Groups of 100 to 200 people would travel by train to northern France to work in the Pas-de-Calais region. No passports or visas were required because the group would travel in special trains run by German soldiers. Once Esther stopped explaining, I thought for a long moment. The whole setup seemed insane, and she agreed.

I thought that the recruiters, who work for the Germans, are probably Nazi sympathizers. How far can I trust them? What can I tell them? I'm only 17, would they notice or even care that I didn't meet their minimum age? The craziest part is how can it make sense for a Jew to be working for the Germans. In a way, signing up seemed like sheer insanity. Hiding in the den of the lion had its obvious advantages – but it also scared me. How could I get away with being surrounded by Germans and not be noticed as a Jew? Wouldn't they notice my dark features and suspect me? No one could get me any good answers to these questions.

For the moment, I was lucky enough to find a place to rest my head and sleep, but sleep would not come. I felt the Nazi noose getting closer to slipping around my neck. If I did nothing at all, I would more than likely end up in a work camp.

Meanwhile, Esther had been searching for a contact to find an authentic-looking false ID. Finally, she found it. It described me as Pieter Lutgert, Dutch citizen, age 20, born in Assen, North Holland. With that false ID card in hand, I summoned up my courage and went to the recruiters to at least feel them out for myself.

My interview was anticlimactic. I walked into a dark, sparsely furnished office. There were no waiting lines and the two recruiters were lounging in their chairs.

"Hi," I said as calmly as I could. "I am Pieter Lutgert and I heard that you could get me a job in France."

"Sure," one of the men said and straightened up in his chair. He seemed friendly and repeated the whole story about the housing, pay, food and work. "We need a lot of people," he concluded, "and the Germans leave everything to us. They are satisfied and happy as long as we furnish workers. They don't check the people we recommend. They pay us regularly and that suggests that the workers we send also will be well paid."

The phrase, "They don't check the people" sounded appealing. Also, the fact that the man specifically mentioned that we would travel by train and cross the Belgian and French borders without being subject to regular checkpoints.

In my mind, I saw a door opening, with a bright light shining through it – but was the bright light a trap? Thoughts like this went through my mind. Finally, I said, "Sounds good, but I want to think it over and clear the idea with my parents."

"Okay," one of the men answered. "But you better make up your mind soon. The next transport leaves in two weeks, and that train is just about full. After that, there won't be another transport for another month."

"I'll get back to you soon," I said and left.

Time was not on my side. I probably had less than a week to make up my mind and take a leap into the unknown. If I didn't go now, I'd have to wait it out for a whole other month. With so many terrible things happening all around me, a month felt like a year, in which the only thing that was likely to happen was that I would be captured.

"God help me," I thought. How can I decide? Should I? Shouldn't I? On the one hand, these recruiters could be exactly who they said they are. On the other hand, they could be a front. Were they setting me up? Day and night, the dilemma troubled my mind.

Esther took great pains to find me hiding places. I also hid at Esther's house from time to time and that, of course, was always the most pleasant for me. One night, we were all together – Esther, me and her mother and brother. We were four, enough people for a spiritual séance.

Setting up for this séance, the four of us sat at a round table. At the edge of the table, they placed small square pieces of cardboard, each marked with one of the letters of the alphabet. After the "Z" were ten additional cards marked from one through ten. In the middle of the table, they placed an upside-down drinking glass, on which the four of us placed our fingers. Incredibly, after a while, the glass started to gyrate, slowly at first and then it spun in wide circles, indicating that a spirit was present.

When the glass started to move, Esther took charge, greeting the presence, "Good evening, who are you?" In response, the glass started moving to several letters to spell something that did not mean anything.

Esther prompted, "Do you have a message?" Now the glass quickly spelled out "Yes" in Dutch.

"Who is the message for?" Esther continued.

My heart skipped a beat when the glass moved in my direction and stopped right in front of me. Instinctively, with trembling voice and butterflies in my stomach, I asked, "Who are you?"

The glass started moving again in wide circles, then suddenly, it went to the B, then E, another E and finally R. I could not breathe anymore. "Uncle Bear?" I yelled incredulously.

"Yes," the glass spelled out. I felt the blood draining from my head and I became dizzy. I was convinced at that moment that Esther had contacted my mother's brother. Our pet name for him was always Uncle Bear.

I was still dazed by the movements of the glass when Esther checked, "Are you Jack's uncle?" Again, the answer was a clear yes, so Esther asked: "Do you have a message for him?"

The glass continued its gyrations until it slowly went to the letter spelled out "Go to France." I could not believe my eyes, and I kept hearing the message in my head – "Go to France" – without truly comprehending what it meant. Finally, I pleaded with her, "Please, help me decide, what should I do?"

"Go with it," she said. "The message we heard came from God." I had never given much thought to God, but the message we heard, and her faith in it, gave me hope. I went back to the recruiters and told them that I had decided to join.

"Good going," they said and added, "Don't worry about anything. Everything will be okay." Did they know? I wondered. Were they sending me a signal? I didn't dare ask.

Now that I made up my mind to go to France, I was getting excited. My doubts returned now and then, but I kept hearing my Uncle Bear's message in my ears:

"Go to France."

Gradually, I let it convince me.

CHAPTER 10

From Holland to France

IN THE FEW days before my departure, Esther comforted me with her advice. When it was time for me to leave, she took me to the track in the Rotterdam station where my train waited. On the platform beside it, we saw a group of men waiting in line. The line moved toward a wide table where the two recruiters who had signed me up sat. They were busily shuffling papers and handing each volunteer a small light blue card.

They gave me mine. It read: "The bearer, *Pieter Lutgert*, is a Dutch national engaged by the German Army to work on the West Wall in France." I followed their directions to put the blue card around my neck.

I nervously looked around for any Germans, but I didn't see any. That put me somewhat at ease, but not for long. I was directed to enter the train three cars to my right. It was full of German soldiers. My heart stood still for a moment, but a young Dutchman from our group told me to walk to the far end of the car. This section contained only Dutch volunteers wearing blue cards, which made me more comfortable.

When the train started moving, I said to myself, "So far, so good. The Germans on this train are just escorting a group of us Dutchmen to France and so far, all is going exactly as promised."

As the train moved slowly through the station, I spotted Esther through a window. With her eyes, she asked if all was okay. I nodded and then her body moved out of sight. The trip started to look like an ordinary train ride.

After several hours, we stopped at the Dutch–Belgian border. I had considered any border crossing a threat but there was no identity control or customs inspection by either Belgian or German officials. After a ten-minute stop, the train rolled on to France.

Crossing the French border was even quicker and less eventful. The two men who had conscripted me had joined us on the train. They came around and explained that we would have a four-to-five-hour stopover in Paris. We would be allowed off the train, be issued an allowance of money, and have permission to go find something to eat.

As the train rolled on, our excitement increased by the minute, and our conversation infected each other. Even the German soldiers, who had kept to themselves, became eager for some conversation. They had trouble understanding Dutch, but we understood their German quite well.

It turned out they didn't know why we were on the train with them. When we told them we were going to help them build the West Wall, they slapped our shoulders and called us "comrades." I stayed out of the conversation as much as possible, and I wasn't the only one. Many of the Dutchmen did not want to fraternize with Germans, despite the fact that we were going to work for them.

Suddenly someone shouted "Look, the Eiffel Tower," and indeed I could make out the hazy outline of the famous structure. It was clear we were getting into Paris.

When we pulled into Gare du Nord, the station for trains from the north, I exulted: "Wow, we are in Paris! I'm in Paris!" Standing among the hundred or so Dutchmen lining up beside the train, I could see French people milling around. They were darkly complected, like me. Perhaps I had made an excellent choice. I looked far more like them than the other Dutchmen, among whom my dark features stuck out like a sore thumb.

The recruiters handed us our allowance and told us to be back by five o'clock sharp. The minute I stepped out of the station, a feeling of freedom and jubilation overwhelmed me. Here I was, walking the majestic avenues of Paris! I no longer was a Jew hounded from place to place, hiding like a criminal. No longer could I be handcuffed, thrown into prison, shot at or demeaned by the enemy.

Here I was, seeing Paris in the springtime. I felt as free as a bird. As I walked along aimlessly, I noticed a familiar name in an announcement on a kiosk: "Django Reinhardt from the Quintette du Hot Club de France playing at La Salle Pleyel." Django was famous for playing guitar using only two functioning fingers. His intricate variations, trills and speed were awe-inspiring and virtually impossible to duplicate. As a kid, I had collected most of his records. Later, I studied guitar with Esther's brother Bram, who pointed out Django's incredible technique.

By amazingly good luck, one of the performances listed on the poster was for that very afternoon, and I still had time to take in the matinee. However, I had no idea where La Salle Pleyel was located. A local told me to take the Metro, transfer at such and such place and walk in such and such direction. Somehow, I got to the concert hall in time to see the show from beginning to end. Hearing him perform live was an experience I shall never forget.

Getting back to the station I got lost several times. But I arrived in time to continue my journey to the southwest coast of France. We arrived at our destination late in the evening. It was dark, but I could see the outlines of barracks. Hundreds of people were milling around, mainly civilians but also German soldiers. Our group was led into a large barracks filled with long, wooden tables and benches. At one end, servers were ladling out hot soup onto metal plates. We sat down and were served along with the rest. The soup tasted surprisingly good, and we got seconds if we asked.

After the meal, they led us to another barracks with a great number of cots against one wall. The other side of the building held lockers for storing personal belongings. Blankets and pillows were stacked in a large bin on top of the lockers.

I selected a bed, made it up and tried to rest, but sleep wouldn't come. I had experienced too much excitement for one day. The lights in our barracks were turned off, but many of the young men were still talking and some were still walking around.

The next morning, I sat down for breakfast in the dining barracks. While I was eating a slice of bread, I noticed someone staring at me. My experience as a Jew in German-occupied territory had made me wary of a stare, and my body would be ready for immediate action. Remarkably, this stare did not alarm me, and I sensed why.

Even in normal times, when two Jewish people meet, they activate a special sense of recognition. Something I couldn't quite describe told me the other person was Jewish and signaled to them that I was Jewish as well. Later that morning he approached me.

"You from Rotterdam?" he asked.

"Sure," I said, "and you?"

"Me too," he answered. "We're both far from home."

"Sure," I said again, still cautious and keeping the conversation short.

We kept looking at each other. He started walking away, but returned abruptly and said, "You know, they are going to examine all newcomers here. We'll all be checked for venereal disease, and a German army doctor who does the checking."

A flash of comprehension went through me and alarm bells started going off in my head. I would stand stripped naked in front of a German doctor. Clearly, this would be a dead giveaway. The old butterflies returned to my stomach. I needed to leave as soon as possible.

The information from the other fellow from Rotterdam was soon confirmed. Over the loudspeaker, we were told that work would not start until the next day, but that we were to report to the medical depot at eight o'clock to be examined.

While I was pondering what to do, one of the men who had recruited me in Rotterdam took me aside and whispered, "I think you should leave. The physical examination tomorrow morning will be made by a German doctor, and people are talking. I doubt this examination would work out well for you."

He never mentioned anything about Jews. He told me to come to his office as soon as possible because there was someone he thought I should meet. When I got there, I was surprised to see that the person was the same fellow to whom I had spoken with earlier. He came close to my ear and said in a low tone "We both have to get out of here as soon as possible, if you understand me, brother."

Cutting straight to the issue, I asked: "You also a Mexican?" He nodded yes. Mexican was Jewish vernacular for "Jewish."

"I'm Piet," I said. "What's yours?"

"Ies," he said. *Ies*, for Isadore, just like the nickname of my brother-in-law who always had treated me so kindly.

Despite the urgency of the situation and the pending danger, I felt good about being with another Ies, a fellow who was Jewish and on the run like me. I also had a good feeling about the recruiter from Holland. I hadn't fooled him one bit. He hired workers to aid the Germans, even though they were the enemy of both the Jews and the Dutch but still he was considered "a Righteous Christian." He had his heart in the right place. He realized I was a Jewish youngster, but he never let on.

"Here," he said, shoving a wad of French francs into one of my pockets, "you'll surely need this."

I did not know how to respond, and tears welled up in my eyes. He more than understood the severity of my situation and cared about the dangers facing me. Back at the barracks, I packed my meager possessions in my small suitcase. My roommates noticed.

"Where are you going?"

"They told me to move to another barracks," I responded. Apparently, that satisfied them.

I met my new-found Jewish friend outside. We decided that too many eyes would be on us if we left during daylight hours. Better to inconspicuously leave at night. We hid our suitcases behind some empty crates. Neither of us had any idea of where we should go.

When it was dark enough, I gave Ies a nod and we picked up our suitcases. Quietly, we walked towards the gate and were surprised to see no guards. It seemed anyone could just leave or enter without being checked. So, we just strolled out and finally had a chance to talk and find out more about each other. Like me, Ies had been in hiding in several places until it became practically impossible to find any new ones. He also had been betrayed and escaped but then found it impossible to stay in German-occupied Holland. Someone had told him that there were people hiring workers for the defenses at the French coast, and he had decided to take his chances, just like me. Ies was considerably older than me, so I thought he might have an idea that I hadn't thought of.

"What are we going to do, Ies?" I asked."

"With our ID from the Germans we might not run into trouble," Ies said brightly, "Even if we should run into somebody." We walked away from the camp, and after about a kilometer and a half, we reached a small village.

"Look, it's late already," Ies said, "Step number one is to find somewhere to sleep."

"Let's go to the church," I suggested, pointing to a shack with a small steeple. "We could ask to speak to the priest. He might find us a place to sleep."

No one was there and the church was locked. We couldn't budge the reddish-brown front door, so we looked for another entrance. Indeed, there was another door at the rear. We rattled that too, and it nearly came apart. We peered inside, and the only thing we saw was a large statue that appeared almost human in the dim light that filtered through two dirty windows. I kept thinking someone was there, watching me and it kept me on edge the whole time.

"Close that door." Ies said. "This is as good as any place to stay for the time being. We won't have to explain ourselves to anybody." I looked inside and said, "I think you're right. It looks safe and that's the main thing. Tomorrow we can tackle the next problem."

We tried to make ourselves as comfortable as possible in that broken-down church. I laid down in one of the pews, put one sheet over me for cover and rolled up another to prop up my head. The pew was narrow and I had to take care not to roll off. While trying to balance ourselves, we drifted in and out of sleep.

A rooster woke us up about 6 a.m. Nothing there to wash our hands and face or to eat for breakfast. The only thing to do was to check out the village. The view made me feel as if I were in the Middle Ages. The buildings, houses and sheds together made up no more than a crossroads. Various farms were scattered around its perimeter. There wasn't a soul to be seen.

We heard voices coming from behind a door with a faded sign that read "Tobacconist." We stepped in and faced a man and woman behind a counter.

"Avez vous quel'que chose a manger?" ("Have you something to eat?") I asked in the best French I could muster. "*Non*," answered the man, they only had "*cafés*." We indicated this would do. When they finally served our coffees, they came in two large white bowls, and the contents didn't look like any coffee I'd ever seen. To me, the French ruin their morning beverage by putting in more milk than coffee. Fine for those who like it, but milk and I are sworn enemies. Luckily, the bread stick that the French serve with their coffee was something I could eat.

CHAPTER 11

Life in Paris

IES AND I made our way back to Paris by train. The trip was a blur. Arriving at Gare du Nord, we saw prostitutes walking the streets and sitting in sidewalk cafés, exposing their legs well above their knees. As a 17-year-old Dutch boy, I was glad to be back in Paris. It was full of new discoveries; men walked arm in arm and kissed on both cheeks in greeting or goodbye. Lovers were openly kissing in public. Things like that would never happen in my conservative Holland. The women, despite shortages of almost everything, were elegantly dressed, and older, gray-haired women had a noticeable dark blue hair tint which made me think of the colors of a parakeet.

Ies and I spotted a hotel across the street from the station named Hotel Belge. This appealed to us because Belgium, bordering Holland, meant they spoke Flemish, a dialect of Dutch. We expected to hear a familiar language and we were right. The owners, Madame Gaston and her son, Michel, spoke Flemish. It gave us a feeling of home. The place was packed with all types of people and teeming with political refugees from Holland and Belgium, mixed with a bevy of thieves, pimps and black marketeers. Everyone was drinking wine, beer or coffee, and creating a blue haze throughout with cigarette smoke – the perfect place for us to blend right in.

Immediately, we were drawn to a group of people who spoke our type of Dutch. After getting into a conversation with them, I noticed Ies was no longer there. I don't know what got into him or what drew him away, but I never saw him again. I suddenly felt very alone.

A group of Dutchmen described how they had left Holland to steer clear of Germans who were forcing people to work in Germany as slave laborers. I was drawn to one of these fellows who said his name was Piet. Piet was tall and scrawny, with black, graying hair and dark, piercing eyes. He was intense. He seemed to take an interest in me and asked how I got to Paris. When I explained how I volunteered to work for the Germans in France he commented, "Smart move."

He described how he had simply walked across the Dutch–Belgian border on a dark night. He moved his hands rapidly as he spoke and his voice was deep. He came across a monastery not far from the border, where a monk helped him find the rest of the way across.

At that, my ears perked up; it sounded like I could count on the clergy for help. Another Dutchman mentioned that several Dutch priests were housed in a religious order on the Left Bank of the city. After some days at the hotel, I decided to find these religious Dutchmen and ask them for support. I left my belongings at the hotel and took the Metro toward the monastery. After getting lost several times, I finally found myself in front of its huge double doors.

On the right side of the door hung a long metal chain with a pear-shaped handle connected to a copper bell. The bell clanged loudly when I yanked the handle, but I had to ring several times before a small window in the door opened. A face stared out at me with small green eyes. The mouth did not say anything, so I decided to state my purpose.

In my best school French, I explained I was a Dutchman and wanted to get in touch with Dutch priests who lived there. Still, the face did not utter a word, but one side of the double door opened and a thin body, wrapped in a priest's robe, motioned me to follow.

He introduced me to Brother Eugene. Tall and slim, with blond hair and blue eyes, he jovially welcomed me in Dutch and asked where in Holland I was from. When I told him, he somehow led the conversation to the treatment of the Jews back home. He thought it was outrageous and went on for a while. Surprisingly soon after, I felt at ease with him. He led me to a quiet corner in one of the study rooms.

Although he never asked me directly, while we were alone, I felt I had to tell him I was Jewish. He looked at me seriously and said he had suspected as much. He sympathized with what I must have gone through and thought the Germans would have a lot to answer for in the end. We left it at that, and he invited me to join him for a hearty meal with the other brothers. Then he assured me I could stay at the monastery for a few days.

After dinner, we talked some more until it was time to go to bed. The monks gave me a small, sparsely furnished, windowless cell. When I lay in bed, ready to sleep, Brother Eugene came to me and placed his hand on my head, and said in a touching tone, "God bless and protect you," and I thanked him. I spent the next day with the Brothers working in their magnificent garden, where they raised a variety of vegetables. I helped dig up potatoes and pick green beans, gathering them in large woven baskets. I had a pleasant time.

After prayers that night, everyone retired. I was tired from all that garden work and lost no time getting undressed. In the middle of this, Brother Eugene entered my room. I had become quite used to him, so I wasn't surprised when he appeared. He had a question for me; he had never seen a circumcised penis before and wondered if I wouldn't mind showing mine to him.

I considered his request as if a doctor had asked me to show my manhood as part of a medical examination. Since I was already in my shorts, I lowered them. Suddenly he flew at me, falling on his knees and grasping my penis in both hands. Shocked, I instinctively drew back and pushed him away. We didn't exchange a word. A deep anger welled up inside me, but I was too embarrassed to say anything. I turned my back and got into bed, and Eugene left.

A little while later, he returned to my room and tried to get under the covers with me. He mumbled embarrassing words. I was able to pull him off me by the black sash that held his robe around his waist. Then, with all my might, I kicked and shoved him out of the bed and onto the floor. I was enraged, but I didn't utter a word even while pushing him out. I had innocently thought I was dealing with a holy man, a sinless being who did not engage in sexual activity.

My trust turned to betrayal. I felt violated, nauseous and unclean; I could not stay at the monastery any longer. Without thinking or reasoning, I got dressed and tried to find the exit in the dark. I had to pass through a labyrinth of hallways before I finally reached the heavy double doors to the outside world.

The only thing that occurred to me to do was return to Hotel Belge. After I checked back in, I didn't go out much. I sat by the window for days and watched the rest of the world go by on Rue St. Quentin. Madame Gaston saw me looking distressed and led me to her back office and fed me some bread, cheese and conversation that took my mind off things.

Seduction

I could tell which women were prostitutes as they were either walking around or sitting on the terraces, heavily made-up, smoking cigarettes and showing off their thighs almost up to their panties. I found it very exciting and sometimes spent hours staring at all the activities. Of course, the young German soldiers on leave were also there, drawn to the prostitutes like bees to honey.

I hadn't seen any German uniforms from my window for a while, and one day I risked venturing out. Strolling near the hotel, I noticed one of the girls staring at me. She was young with blonde, curly hair that reminded me of Shirley Temple. She had a baby face with blue eyes and a round pouting mouth. I kept looking at her cherry red lips. A few days later, I almost bumped into her when I turned a corner near the hotel.

"Hi, I'm alone tonight," poured out of my mouth in French. The language was becoming easier and those words were on my mind because of the lyrics to a popular song.

"Me too," she said.

The blonde and I quickly were on the same wavelength, and I indicated that I wanted to take her to my room. She signaled her agreement by taking my arm under hers and squeezing it while we walked upstairs.

Her name was Solange, and she was just starting out in her profession. We spent two full days in my room with only a bottle of cheap wine. We'd only leave to buy some *tartes aux flammes* at a nearby patisserie to fill our hungry stomachs and reenergize. We'd rapidly return to our room to continue our lovemaking.

Solange never asked me for money. It never occurred to me to pay her. She said she loved me and, I don't know why, but she called me "*Mon petit Americain*." Then she announced she was going to "work" for me. I had no income and little money left, so the idea appealed to me at first. However, when I considered it in earnest, I decided being a pimp was not the job for me. When I told her so, she got angry and left after a lot of screaming and throwing things around. I thought I'd seen the last of her until a week later she woke me up in the middle of the night and threw a bunch of crumpled francs on my bed.

"It's for you, chéri, I work for you," she repeated. I was half asleep and did not immediately realize what was happening. Groggily, I turned on the light and took a good look at her. Her face was gray, with deep circles under her eyes and her hair was disheveled.

I was appalled at what her work had done to her in so short a time, and my dismay got worse when I smelled alcohol on her breath. My eyes darted from her pallid appearance to the money she had flung onto the bed. Despite the fact the money was very tempting, once it sank in how the money was acquired, my stomach turned. The sexual attraction I once had vanished and turned into revulsion.

She started to undress and wanted to get into bed with me. I got flustered, jumped up, instinctively pulled off the top sheet and tried to hide my naked body from her. The scene got uglier. She started screeching, screaming and crying. As her shrieks increased, I got panicky. I could feel the old butterflies in my stomach returning. Butterflies that were always with me day and night in Holland, when hiding or running from the Nazis. I dressed as fast as I could, ran out of the room, jumped down the stairs, crossed the lobby and hit the street.

I stayed away from the hotel for two full days, afraid of running into Solange, and worrying about the meager possessions I had left in my room. When I returned, to my great surprise, all the money she had thrown on the bed lay there untouched. She had left no signs that she was still around.

I picked up the cash and headed downstairs. In crossing the lobby, I met one of the Dutchmen who frequented the place, the same one I had met the day I arrived. The French called him Pierre and the Dutch called him Pieter, or Piet for short. With the few hundred windfall francs in my pocket, I felt generous and treated him to an afternoon apéritif.

While we sipped our drinks, I told him I had acquired the money because a prostitute I was seeing had insisted on "working for me." He began laughing incredulously. He thought I was being too choosy, turning down a sweet deal to make good money. He wondered how I expected to keep on going, reasoning that the money she earned would be safe. I let him know the very idea filled me with disgust.

"Well, have it your way," he said. "I wish that I could land a sweet deal like that. What I have to do to earn a living pays well, but it's far more difficult and dangerous." I told him I wanted to know more. He lowered his voice and whispered the details, describing a contact of his who works for the Germans. It was in one of their storage facilities full of supplies like food, uniforms, socks, underwear, boots and tools.

I asked him if the fellow was a German collaborator and he explained he was a guy like us, who needed a job. He loathed the Germans and sabotaged them whenever he could. In fact, he purposely hid supplies so he could smuggle them out. Sometimes he hid items in the trash and then hauled it out the back door once the coast was clear. He started small, and when no one noticed, he hid a whole lot more. So, besides his salary, a new source of income opened for him.

I asked Piet how he was involved and he looked around and continued in hushed tones explaining the contact offered him a deal. After the stuff was stockpiled and the garbage hauled out to a safe place, he would then retrieve it and sell the goods. The two of them shared in the profits.

He explained it was operationally easy to pull off as the French had shortages of everything. Customers were willing to buy without question, even if they sensed that what they were buying were black-market goods. Last week he landed a great deal of money when he sold a whole load of socks to a guy who resold them at a flea market. On hearing this, I told him I was interested to get in on the deal. It would further reduce their risk and together we could move more goods. Piet reminded me it was still a dangerous venture, but I told him I was ready to start right away.

He said he was expecting a load of work boots in a few days, offering to show me a sample that was in his room. I told him we could trust each other. We were friends, both from Holland, and I could pay him ahead of time for the lot with the money I got from Solange, so he didn't have to worry about waiting until the stuff was sold. He agreed and took me up to his room to show me the sample boot he kept hidden. It looked like good quality.

The next day I did some sniffing around. I knew someone who operated a shoe store who was deemed reliable and when I looked him up, he seemed most anxious to buy the boots. He said to bring him all I could get because he could probably sell it all in a single day.

A few days later, there was a knock on my door. At first, I was afraid it might be Solange, but once I heard Piet's voice I let him in. The plan was in progress as promised. He explained there was a load of boots that would be packed into a box easy enough to be carried away. He wanted 400 francs for the lot, which could easily be sold for 100 francs each. My guy at the shoe store had already mentioned the same price, so everything was coming together nicely.

He told me to meet him at the corner of Boulevards Magenta and Haussmann at 8 p.m. that night to pick up the box. I gave him the money and we shook hands, sealing the deal. When the door closed behind him, I started envisioning all the money I'd earn, dreaming of what I'd do with it. I was feeling good and considered myself a pretty smart cookie.

It was still many hours before our scheduled meeting, but I was nervous and impatient. In my mind, I was already rich, so I treated myself to a sumptuous meal at one of the small restaurants in the area. I loved the brie they served for dessert. They also did shady business, so they did not ask for the ration tickets restaurants were required to collect.

The afternoon dragged on. As the hands of the restaurant's clock moved closer toward eight o'clock, I couldn't sit still anymore, and I arrived at the appointed corner 20 minutes ahead of time. I walked around a bit, watching the crowd on the busy boulevard. It was getting dark and because of the blackout mandated by the German occupation, no streetlights came on. In the semi-dark, about five minutes to eight, my eye caught something suspicious on the other side of the street.

A black car stopped at the curb. Four men descended, crossed over and walked towards the corner where I was supposed to meet Piet. I was surrounded by pedestrians, so while I could see the men, they couldn't spot me. Carefully I edged closer, and then clearly recognized Piet, but the three guys with him just didn't seem right and none of them carried a box.

Piet spotted me, and suddenly they all started running fast toward me. They looked at me as if I were the target. I couldn't believe this had turned into a set-up! As I raced down the boulevard with enormous power, the pedestrian traffic thickened, and I knew I was hard to track as I dodged between people. I was trying to run fast while avoiding pedestrians. My mind was on high alert when I slammed head-on into an old lady so forcefully her small hat flew off her head, revealing the noticeable blue tinge in her gray hair. She crashed to the pavement on her back.

I felt terrible for having hurt the old lady, but I didn't have much choice. I had to keep running until I felt that no one was following me. I finally stopped to sit down on a stoop and tried to make sense of what had happened. Piet, who was supposed to be my friend, turned out to be a collaborator. He must have been working with either the German or the French police. Either way, I hoped they gave him plenty of trouble seeing how he missed the opportunity to catch me.

I got angry beyond words. *Wait till I get my hands on that traitor*, I thought, *I'll wring his neck!* But I realized he had the advantage – he knew where to find me. In effect, he's deprived me of the only relatively safe place I knew, Hotel Belge. Surely Piet and his goons were planning to catch me there next. I no longer knew who I could trust and all my money was gone. I felt like I was running out of options. What now? Where would I go?

I decided to take the Metro as far as it would go and rode to the end of the line at Montmartre. That seemed far enough. I found a small hotel on Rue du Cherche-Midi, not exactly knowing where I was. When I woke up the next morning, I found myself staring at the rear of the Sacré-Cœur Basilica through a small window in my room. Piet's betrayal would not leave my mind. I kept dreaming up scenarios to get even with him. I even considered outright killing him but abandoned the idea. I didn't have it in me, and he wasn't worth the trouble.

I had to wait it out but eventually I needed to pick up the few belongings I had left in my room at Hotel Belge. I particularly wanted to shave and get into some clean clothes, so I lasted as long as my patience allowed. I made my way back but kept an eye out for any police or anyone suspicious. Around midnight, I hadn't spotted anything unusual and from my spot across the street I noticed Michel sitting at the reception desk, so I went up and asked if he'd seen my friend, Piet. He delivered the best news possible; Piet had moved out with all his belongings.

I went back to stay at the hotel at Rue du Cherche-Midi and stayed in my room until I came up with a plan. I felt safer there, but whenever I went out, I always checked to see if I was watched or followed. In the end, I realized I needed to consult my only dependable friends in Paris, the owners of Hotel Belge. I took the chance and went back, hoping the coast was clear. I cautiously approached the hotel once it seemed safe.

"My God. Pierre, is it you?" Madame Gaston exclaimed as I entered the reception area, "I was hoping you'd be alright."

She'd learned about the set-up from Michel, and she let me know the police had come by asking for both Piet and me. Of course, she said she didn't let on that she had known anything. I thanked her for the update and explained I came back to follow up on her suggestion to get out of Paris, where it was obviously getting too dangerous for me. She agreed and suggested I leave soon and stay away for a long time.

Madame Gaston had an idea, she wanted to connect me to some trustworthy friends by the name of Van Houtte, people as Dutch as their name sounded and "friendly to our cause." They had a lot of "good connections," which was the understood code for, anti-German friends. She would contact them and let them know I was coming. She gave me their address, suggesting I waste no time in getting there.

CHAPTER 12

A Miracle in Auxerre

I HEADED TO the end of the Metro line at Château de Vincennes, an upscale suburb. As I walked from the station, I passed expensive homes with oak and chestnut trees lining the avenues. The Van Houtte residence was impressive. When I knocked on the massive oak double doors and stated my name, the brass handles turned and a man led me into the entrance hall.

Jules van Houtte was a tall, slender man with graying temples; his wife was an attractive, classic blonde lady. Both greeted me enthusiastically in Dutch and were anxious to hear what I could tell them about Holland, especially how Dutch and German Nazis were plundering our country. When I spoke of the horrendous treatment of the Jews, Mrs. Van Houtte looked at me tearfully and said her heart went out to me and figured that my being Jewish had sent me to them.

Her words felt like stabs in my heart. Her sobs brought back the many months of running and hiding from the Germans and everything I had been through. I trusted the Van Houttes fully. All caution and secrecy went out the window, and I told them about the dangers I had faced. When they asked how old I was, I told them the truth. I was 17, I had a fake identity and was alone with no idea where my parents and sisters were.

They knew I needed to get out of Paris. I told them my dream of becoming a pilot so I could bomb the Germans, but they quickly reminded me that the Germans were shooting down too many planes out of the sky and I had to admit they were right. We talked deep into the night. I so appreciated the warm ambiance of their home and their open friendliness that I wanted to stay as long as possible. They told me to return once they had made some inquiries on my behalf.

It didn't take long for our next get-together, when they announced they had already arranged a contact for me; a Dutch farmer in Auxerre, a tiny village in the middle of nowhere. There were no Germans around for miles, so it would be safe to wait out the rest of the war there. The farmer had offered that I could work on the farm in exchange for room and board.

Since I had no idea how to reach Auxerre, Mrs. Van Houtte wrote instructions on a small piece of paper detailing the route from the Gare de l'Est station to the farm. I still seemed unsure, so in her tiny handwriting, she drew a precise map for me on a piece of paper.

When I said my goodbyes to my trusted friends at Hotel Belge and rounded up what little possessions I had, I was feeling hopeful. I wasn't too concerned about identity checks on the train because I still had the blue pass from the West Wall work crew that officially identified me as Pieter Lutgert. After two uneventful hours on the train, I arrived at Auxerre station, which looked like a broken-down shed.

All seemed peaceful until I walked along the short road from the station toward the exit. To my consternation, I saw that French State Police and German soldiers had set up a checkpoint, to examine those heading to the exit. From the way the line moved, I got the impression they were doing a routine ID check rather than a thorough grilling. I surveyed the situation. Running away was out of the question. Not only was there nowhere to run, but it also would be too obvious. I told myself to act normal, but it was hard to deal with the butterflies in my stomach.

The first gendarme who confronted me didn't ask for papers but held out his hand. For a split second, I thought I was supposed to shake it but quickly abandoned the idea. I put my blue pass into his outstretched hand. He was French, and because the pass was written in German and Dutch, he couldn't make sense of it.

In my still broken French, I tried to explain that I was a Dutchman who worked for the German Army. He still looked puzzled, so on impulse, I turned to one of the German soldiers and in my best German mixed with Dutch I asked him to please tell these "French idiots" that I worked for them. He completely ignored the pass and told me he had nothing to do with civil matters. He wore a metal breastplate that I later learned identified him as military police. He only dealt with German army personnel.

All four Frenchmen jumped on me and grabbed my small suitcase. It held all my worldly possessions – a few magazines, toiletries, underwear and an electric shaver. They searched it and spilled out its contents, including the small map that Mrs. Van Houtte had made for me.

Pointing to the map, they challenged me to explain what it was. I pretended not to understand the question while trying to devise a reason for being this deep in the French interior. If I were supposedly employed by the West Wall fortifications, why would I be carrying a map that led to a seemingly unrelated destination in Auxerre?

Finally, I put on a look of understanding their questions, and said as nonchalantly as I could that I was on vacation and came to look up an old friend. One of the Frenchmen sharply uttered a single word: "*Espion*."

I understood exactly what that word meant: spy. Accusing me of being a spy produced a grave reaction that sent chills up my spine. In my mind's eye, I saw myself in front of a firing squad ready for execution. The two of them escorted me to their headquarters and started interrogating me.

The questioning went from routine – "Where are you from and where are you going?" – to, "What is your real mission? What's your real name? Which base are you from in England? Who is your contact in France?" The interrogation went on for hours. The more I denied being a spy from England, the more they intensified their questioning. Abruptly, they stopped and pushed me into a dark room without windows. I could hear the lock on the door click behind me.

Nothing happened for hours. I couldn't believe I was accused of being a spy, and I couldn't figure out why. I tried to force the door open a hundred times without success. I had no option but to sit on a hard wooden bench and wait. A thousand frightening thoughts ran through my head, worsened by darkness and silence. It felt as if the whole building had been abandoned and I was the only living soul inside. The unknown terrified me, and I was sure my end was near.

I was half dazed when the door suddenly flung open. In the semi-darkness, I saw a uniformed man beckoning me to get up and follow him. When he spoke, he said he was taking me to see the chief and that I had better tell the truth. As menacing as it sounded, I was too numb and confused to feel much. I still couldn't understand why they were insisting I was a spy. It seemed to be all because of the hand-drawn map, but nothing made sense. The man brought me to a brightly lit office and I stumbled inside.

When my eyes adjusted, I saw a man sitting behind a desk resembling an upside-down wooden box. His long legs were sticking out through an opening in the middle. He wore the khaki uniform of the French State Police, and a black beret sat askew on his gray hair. My small suitcase sat on top of his desk; beside it lay my two magazines, underwear, comb, hairbrush, electric razor and the map – that damning piece of paper that might lead me to a firing squad instead of a simple Dutch farmer.

The policeman picked it up with his thumb and forefinger, letting it hang loosely in front of my face and asked, "*Qu'est-ce que c'est ca*?" What is this? There was no point in pretending I was a Dutchman on vacation from German Army duties on his way to look up an old friend in Auxerre. This story hadn't made sense to any previous interrogator. I took a new tack and explained the map was supposed to take me to a Dutch farmer who needed a farmhand. My friends in Paris had given me the map to help me find my way there.

"Why would a Dutch boy like you want to work on a farm in Auxerre?" he challenged point blank. I took a moment to think and explained that back in Holland, I was afraid they'd take me to Germany to work, so I came here where I was told they left farm boys alone. Because there was some partial truth to this, it seemed to strike him as more credible, so I went on.

I explained we had bad luck back home. My father remained disabled from a plowing accident and could no longer work. He wanted me to take over the farm and once I learned enough and had the necessary experience, I could. I looked up and added, "So you see sir, it's not really complicated and I am telling you the truth."

I was spinning a story that flowed out of my mouth so fluently and earnestly that it even surprised me, considering my French was nothing to brag about. In fact, my French was ramshackle, interrupted that by numerous "uhs" and long hesitations while I desperately searched for words.

The man behind the desk seemed to think for a while when I stopped speaking. Then, looking straight into my eyes, he plainly said, "Young man, I personally don't believe your story; it all sounds made up to me. You don't look like a farmer, nor does it seem like you come from a family of farmers. My colleagues and I think you're a spy from England that dropped out of the sky. That is where our heads are at, but I also believe you have something else to hide and I intend to find out what it is."

I didn't understand what he was talking about and all I could think to do was stick to my story. I swore it was the truth. I didn't dare tell the real truth – that I was a Jewish kid on the run from the Nazis. He didn't let up and the interrogation went on. I became dizzy and the room started to spin. I was overwhelmed by the mental strain of seeking French words and the fear of being discovered as a Jew. I broke out in a cold sweat from mental stress and exhaustion. To keep standing, I held onto the edge of his desk. As he rose from behind it, his over-six-foot frame towered over me.

"Well kid, I have an idea what you're hiding from me, but I'm not going to push you any further. Instead, I have some good advice for you." As he spoke, he took me by the collar and led me to a room. Through the window, I could see we were at the back of the building, facing a deep clearing and, beyond that, a forest. He opened a side door, shoved my blue ID card into my clammy hand and went on. "Young man, this is my advice: get away from here and run as fast as your legs can carry you. Run!"

The fresh cool night air hit my overheated face. My brain tried to understand what had just happened, did I hear right? Did he tell me to "run away from here?" Was I hallucinating? Was it an excuse to shoot me in the back while I was running? I felt like a condemned man with a noose around his neck, expecting a trap door to open and then ... nothing happened. No drop, no gagging, no breaking the bones of my neck.

All that flashed through my head in a split second. Then my legs found the ground and I started running as if pursued by the devil. No shot was fired, no one chased after me. Somehow, I made it back to Paris, but I don't remember how. The whole return trip was a blur in my mind.

CHAPTER 13

Hope of a New Life

WITH THE AUXERRE adventure behind me, and having been back in Paris for a few weeks, it was time that I informed the Van Houttes about my state of affairs. They didn't know I was back in Paris or that trying to get the job in Auxerre was a disaster.

When I hurried to their home in the early afternoon, they were happy and very surprised to see me. With eyes wide in disbelief, they listened to my incredible escape from the dreaded French gendarmerie.

"It's unbelievable. Unbelievable." they kept repeating. They knew the French traitors to be infamous for their cruelty and were relieved I had encountered someone who was on our side. We found out the reason I had raised suspicions at that checkpoint was because British parachutists had been seen landing in Auxerre a few days before, and half the French police and many units of the German army were patrolling, looking to capture them. I also had found out those unlucky enough to be imprisoned there were tortured. It was pure bad luck that I had arrived at that particular time in that ordinary, tranquil, small town.

Fortunately, the chief of the French gendarmerie who interrogated me was no Nazi sympathizer like the rest. He must have guessed I was Jewish even though I tried to hide it. He took a big risk in helping me, and he must have had to make up his own fancy story to explain to the other gendarmes what had become of me.

The Van Houttes promised to connect me with one of their contacts that would find a good place for me to stay, away from Paris. The city had become too full of Nazi spies, and they thought it would only be a matter of time until they caught up with me. It had become too dangerous.

Again, I had to agree. As the war and German occupation dragged on, stories of Nazi raids on Jewish homes were abundant and young men were being randomly picked up on the streets. Upon leaving, I promised to stay in touch. Mrs. Van Houtte, in turn, promised to contact Madame Gaston or her son as soon as they had found a suitable place for me in the countryside. She urged me to be careful. I should be prepared to get out of Paris, it wouldn't be long now, they assured me and then she hugged me goodbye.

The following weeks were pure agony. Yet, the fact I had not yet found the Dutchman, Piet for payback was starting to nag me. In my mind, I blamed the Dutchman Piet for everything that had happened to me. I had no money, since he made off with my 400 francs. I could have sold the stolen German boots for a big profit. Had he not run off with my money and tried to turn me over to the police, I wouldn't have had to go to Auxerre, where all these nasty things happened to me. The more I thought about how I believed the unrealistic scenario, the more it infuriated me. I totally ignored the fact that the black-market boots probably never even existed and were simply bait to get me arrested.

It was 2:00 a.m. one morning when I considered it safe enough to return to the Hotel Belge, hoping the police wouldn't be on the lookout for me so early. There was no one behind the reception desk, so I went into the little office behind the bar where I found Michel half-asleep and almost sliding off a broken-down chair. Once he realized it was me, I got his attention immediately,

"Where have you been?" He asked. He and Madame Gaston were afraid the police or Germans had picked me up. When I told him what had happened in Auxerre, he couldn't believe his ears. He said it was a miracle I came out alive. He insisted I was a very lucky fellow because he hadn't known many people who got away from "those bastard French State Police, who were all Goddamned Nazis." He produced a bottle of cheap red pinot, uncorked it, and got two dirty tumblers from a ledge that sat near the floor in an even dirtier cabinet. Pouring the tumblers full to the rim he yelled, "To victory and to your lucky star!"

The pinot was soon gone with Michel being the recipient of the lion's share. He produced a second bottle which he started to uncork. I did not particularly like the taste of wine and was not a big drinker; one glass was more than enough to make me dizzy. I held my hand over the dirty tumbler, refusing any more. Well into the second bottle, he confided that about a week ago, two men in civilian clothes who identified themselves as police questioned his mother about a "certain Pierre, a Dutchman." She acted as if she didn't know me and they left.

He became somber and recommended I get away from there as soon as possible. He didn't want me to be foolish because I'd been lucky so far, and he didn't want me to count on being protected forever. Michel urged me to forget about getting even with the Dutch traitor; his time would come once the war was over. I realized despite my strong desire to get even with Piet, I ran a great risk of getting myself caught. It wasn't worth it.

I headed back to my hotel back at Rue du Cherche-Midi while it was still dark. Once I got to my room, my dreams were rudely interrupted by the concierge of the hotel. I didn't know her name but I hated her the moment I'd laid eyes on her. She had a skeletal face with gaunt skin. Her bulging eyes had the same gray color as her hair. This woman was a look-alike of a real witch; the only thing missing was her broomstick. Through the door, she began demanding the rent, reminding me I was almost a week late.

"Yes I know," I replied. I said I was sorry. I explained that because I'd been so busy with work, I'd completely forgot about it and I'd have the money for her tomorrow after going to the bank. She sounded satisfied and shuffled away without a word.

I didn't sleep long and woke up extra early to rush back to Hotel Belge, anxious to find out if they had heard from the Van Houttes. The reception area was full of people, but I didn't see Michel or his mother. I located the assistant manager on duty, Sebastian, a virulent anti-Nazi who knew what had happened to me. He whispered for me to come back tonight as Michel and his mother were off duty but back after eight o'clock. He believed they had news for me.

It sounded good so I rushed back to my hotel, rather than risk staying outside with the possibility of being spotted by police. When it was dark and almost eight o'clock, I took the Metro back to Hotel Belge where I hoped to get news from my friends. The minute I entered the lobby I saw Madame Gaston behind the reception counter, she was busy speaking to a man, but when she saw me, a big smile spread across her face. She indicated with her outstretched hand to go to the small back office where I found Michel.

His eyes were wide when he told me I was all set. The Van Houttes had found a safe place for me in a small village called Pamfou. A Dutch farmer was willing to hire me in exchange for room and board, his name was Jan Suurd and the farm was about 70 kilometers south of Paris. Upon hearing this wonderful news, I grabbed Michel by the shoulders and we both danced around his small office, almost knocking over the furniture.

Traveling back to my hotel that same night, I waited until the "witch" was no longer behind the reception. The main entrance door was locked. Cautiously I turned the lever and opened the door. I slipped out unnoticed extra early in the morning, making another escape to a new life of farming.

As I entered the bus station headed in the direction of Place Jean-Jaurès, I tried to blend in with the other travelers on the platforms. I was tense and ready to dodge any threatening movement that came my way. It seemed as though the coast was clear and I saw my bus, marked "Montreux." I had rehearsed the schedule to avoid carrying a map. First stop was Melun and then Pamfou, located in the Seine-et-Marne district.

CHAPTER 14

Pamfou — Life in the Country

AFTER JUST AN hour and a half, the bus stopped in front of a restaurant at a crossroads. With no map, I needed to ask for directions. When I entered the restaurant, I got the attention of the man behind the bar and asked in my best French if he knew how I could find the red farm that belonged to the Dutchman, Jan Suurd.

He told me the farm was about one kilometer north, but the farmer didn't live there; he and his family resided in the house right behind this restaurant. All I had to do was turn left at the corner and their house would be right there.

I thanked him and shortly thereafter I was standing in front of the Suurds' door and knocked. The woman who answered addressed me in a funny language that sounded neither French nor Dutch. Realizing I did not understand her, she laughed and said in fluent Dutch, "I see, you're not Frisian; you're from Holland."

I told her I was confused because I was Dutch and thought she was from Holland as well, but she explained that her people considered themselves from Friesland, not Holland. They called themselves and their language Frisian. I knew Friesland was one of the 12 Dutch provinces. She managed a wry smile and said they'd been expecting me.

I introduced myself as Pieter Lutgert and she invited me into a large kitchen with a wooden table in the center. She introduced herself as, Anje Suurd. I looked her over while she talked. Anje Suurd was at least six feet tall, and her skinny figure made her look even taller. She had white skin that contrasted intensely with her black hair. Her hair was combed tightly back, forming a bun on the back of her head. Two grayish-blue eyes peered from her long face which, together with her sharp nose, made her look like a stern schoolteacher.

Anje explained that her husband, Jan, and the boys would be coming home for supper around six or seven o'clock from working in the field not far from here. Soon after, a chubby, short young girl walked into the kitchen. Anje introduced her as her sister-in-law, Berta. Berta seemed shy and whispered something I couldn't understand.

Anje had a crisp manner of speaking and in a half-nasal voice, she asked many questions about my background. I didn't risk telling her any truth about myself. I made up a story that I was a high school student whose parents had foreseen the dangers the Germans would pose for young men.

I embellished further, claiming they spent a lot of money trying to get me into neutral Switzerland, but the plan had failed. I explained that luckily, it worked out for my two sisters and mother, who were now safely there. I explained my dad was okay in Holland as he was a businessman, managing two stores. I thought the story sounded reasonably plausible, and I didn't care whether she believed me or not.

Anje led me to a room on the second floor where I would sleep. It was sparse and had a single window. Beneath the window was a bare wooden table with a chair on the side. The simple wrought-iron bed was unmade and revealed a very thin mattress. The whole place looked and felt barren and cold.

Around 7 p.m. all the men arrived at the home. Anje's husband, Jan was a jovial man with a round face and ruddy complexion. It was obvious he was the boss. His younger brother, Klaas, also ruddy with a freckled face, was married to Berta. Jens, a scrawny redhead with a nondescript expression, was next in line, while Hans, the youngest of Jan's three brothers, looked like a cherub.

All of them seemed pleased that I'd come to help, and we exchanged many pleasantries. Of course, they wanted to know who, what, where and how, so I repeated my made-up history. I never even came close to saying anything that had anything to do with Jews.

When it was time for dinner, we all sat down around the wooden table in the kitchen with Jan Suurd at the head. Then came an embarrassing moment. I noticed a Bible in front of him, and everyone bowed their heads and folded their hands in prayer. I didn't know how to react. Instinctively I folded my hands, closed my eyes and bowed my head as well. That seemed to be enough.

We didn't need to do anything but listen to Jan read from the Bible, which lasted about five to ten minutes. We also listened when next Jan closed his eyes and incanted a hymn. And finally, Anje and Berta served what they called dinner. The food was tasteless except for the green beans, which were sour. There was also a jar on the table containing a grayish liquid that turned out to be the gravy for the very bland potatoes.

Everyone served themself in an orderly manner starting with Jan, who passed each dish to the person sitting next to him, continuing around the table. I wolfed down the lousy food, having not eaten anything all day. A short thank you prayer followed when all had cleaned their plates.

At night, I curled up in my cold room and fell into a deep sleep. At 5 a.m., exhausted, I was rudely awakened by a loud voice from downstairs: "Time to get up, Pieter!" I shook myself awake and dressed hastily, not bothering to wash up or brush my teeth. I didn't want to be late on my first day. When I rushed downstairs expecting to find everyone sitting around the breakfast table, the only one in sight was Anje.

I was astonished and asked where everyone was. She explained the men were already making their way to take care of the animals. When those chores were done, we could come back for breakfast. I ran after the men and followed them to the farm, about a 15-minute walk along a dirt road. There, I was introduced to the two work horses, Gamin, a male, and Papillon, a mare. Jan put them in my care and gave me a special brush to scrub them every morning. He warned me to watch for horse flies.

I looked up in surprise. He said they usually attack the animal on the upper part of the back, out of reach of their tail. I asked if they did a lot of harm and he warned me to look out for open wounds that I would have to tend to. Swatting the flies wouldn't be hard, he explained, because they sucked up so much blood that they were almost too heavy to fly away.

Next, Jan showed me how to clean the stable. I had to remove the old straw and replace it with fresh stuff from the loft, then feed the horses some hay and fill their bins with oats. I tried to follow all these directions. The work was strange to me and took me a couple of hours. By the time we all returned to the house, I was tired and famished. However, before I could start eating, Jan Suurd launched into another ten minutes of Bible reading and prayer.

After the last Amen, Anje came in with breakfast, assisted by Berta. They dumped a grayish liquid onto my plate — watery oatmeal with no taste. The only thing that was pleasant to eat was the white bread that came from Anje's oven, and luckily there was plenty of it. There was no milk, butter or sugar on the table. They had a steaming red urn that seemed to hold coffee, but instead contained a weird brew made from roasted grain that looked and tasted like mud.

We worked all day until dusk. Upon returning to the house, Anje and Berta brought out more of their terrible food. Again, none of it touched our lips until Jan Suurd had finished his prayers. I stuffed myself with dry potatoes and white bread, the only two things that didn't make me nauseous. Then I crawled upstairs to my room and instantly fell into a deep, dreamless sleep.

Each successive day seemed a repetition of the first. Work, work, work — digging up potatoes, a back-breaking job; plucking green beans from their stalks; cleaning out the stables; feeding the horses and cows; hauling things from one place to another; watering plants; hoeing weeds — on and on, paralyzing my arms. What bothered me the most was that it wore big holes in the only pair of shoes I possessed, and they practically fell apart.

I found out that to get a new pair of shoes you had to have a ration card. I didn't have one, but it didn't matter because the stores in town had no shoes to sell anyway. The Suurds wore *klompen*, wooden shoes, and they suggested I try them. After a few hours in the field, I had to take them off. They tired my legs and caused painful blisters on the tops of my feet. The soles of my feet were already sore from tiny cuts and gashes from the grit and dirt that had slipped into the holes of my old shoes. Soon, I was no longer able to walk. I had to stay in my room for a whole week, nursing my infected feet with warm, wet towels.

When I healed some, I couldn't face wearing my torn old shoes again. I was helped by a part-timer who occasionally worked on the farm. His name was Bernard, a boy of about 15 and, being three years older, I called him "my little friend." He was not very tall, but he had strong hands. He had filled in to take on some of my share of the work and when we worked together, he showed me how to do my tasks with less strain. When he noticed my despair about my torn shoes, he went home and returned with a pair of used work boots. They had seen better days, but they were heaven compared to the hell caused by what I had been wearing.

He told me I could keep them because they belonged to his father who had received new ones. After telling his father about me, he wanted me to have them. This was the best gift I could wish for. I let Bernard know I didn't know how to thank him enough and slapped him on the back in sincere appreciation.

My other big problem was the lousy food the Suurd family kept serving. The ingredients were unvaryingly the same, every day of the week, for months on end. With the hard work and lousy food, I started to seriously lose weight.

One day, the issue of my background came up again. I didn't reveal much more when Jan asked to see my old Dutch identification card I carried. When I brought it out, he let out a "*Hmmm ...*" I didn't know what that meant. Surely, he couldn't know Pieter Lutgert wasn't my real name and that the whole thing was a forgery.

He gave it back and launched into a related story of his own. He had arrived from Holland in 1938, when Dutch farmers were very sought-after. The town's officials classified him as a master agricultural expert and issued him identification papers granting special privileges. One such benefit was permission to operate a farm and to hire and train farmhands. He winked at me, indicating I was lucky to be one of these farmhands.

Jan explained he could also get me a better ID than what I had now. It was called a "*laissez-passer*," a permit of official authorization that would fully legitimize me as a worker on his farm with official status. That sounded good to me; I told him I would be very grateful. However, I grew concerned and nervous when Jan told me to prepare to travel with him by bus to the police station in Montreux. I feared that somehow the police might have information about my activities in Paris.

After a two-hour bus trip, we entered the station. I was quite anxious, which I tried to hide, but Suurd noticed and told me not to worry. It was a simple formality. They took a picture of me, and I signed the application that was officially going to make me Pieter Lutgert. When all the paperwork was done, they handed me my official *laissez-passer* for signature and official stamps. After that, they placed it in a gray envelope that contained several other documents and handed it to Jan Suurd. Since he was my official employer, all documents were to be delivered to him, they explained. I had no problem with this, because right after Jan handed me my *laissez-passer*, my identity completely changed and evidence of my Jewish past was erased.

CHAPTER 15

Into the Woods

IN GERMAN-OCCUPIED FRANCE, the mail service was censored. Sometimes it took weeks or months for a letter to arrive at its destination; sometimes it never arrived at all. But occasionally I received letters from Esther. A recent one hinted she was in some kind of danger, so I made a bold decision to return to Rotterdam and see her in person to understand what the trouble was. I was young, daring, physically strong and in love, plus I now had official papers that protected me. I saw myself as a knight in shining armor riding off to her rescue.

Instead of a horse, this knight took a train from Paris to Northern France. There, I found a priest who smuggled me into Belgium. When I reached the Dutch border, local smugglers guided me into a very dangerous occupied Holland. Soon I found myself in the arms of a surprised Esther, who could not believe her eyes when I arrived.

Her safety in Holland had expired. The fact she was only half-Jewish no longer protected her, as restrictions on Jews had intensified. The arrest and disappearance of her father also made her a target. I had to take Esther back to Pamfou with me, so I used the same ploys to avoid interrogation at the borders. My newly acquired *laissez-passer* gave me confidence. I pinned all my hopes on it to work, and it did. We were never stopped once, and even though I knew it was reckless, I was able to pull it off. I was lucky to be out of Holland and Paris, and now Esther was safe with me.

I introduced her as my wife to the Suurds. Whether or not they believed me I could not tell, but they took her in without question and she started to help in the kitchen to the delight of Anje and Berta. Things were back to the rigorous daily routine on the farm. Then one day while working in the field with my friend Bernard, I was shocked to see him munching on a piece of chocolate. Stunned and salivating, I had no idea you could get chocolate at a time like this. He explained that it was easy – all I had to do was give my chocolate ration coupon to the butcher when it came in and he would give me some. He would also exchange groceries and other rationed stuff with the other coupons.

I told him I didn't understand; the only thing I had was the *laissez-passer* Suurd helped me get. I never saw a ration card. But Bernard insisted it made no sense, because you would automatically get a ration card with your *laissez-passer*. I began to realize something did not add up. I remembered that Suurd received a gray envelope with documents in it when we were at the police station. That's who had my ration card! He must've been cashing in my rations on the black market this whole time.

When I confronted Jan Suurd and asked why I never saw any chocolate, butter or cheese on the table, his feeble answer was that by the time his wife got to the store, those things were sold out. I said I didn't believe him and demanded my ration card. He tried giving me all sorts of reasons – he couldn't find it, his wife had it, it wasn't really mine, and so on.

It turned into a big argument. When my temper shot into overdrive, he suddenly "found" my ration card. It clearly indicated the coupons were all used up to the current month. All this time he was selling my rations and I was forced to eat that horrible food day after day.

This discovery made me realize how miserable I was working and living with the Suurd family. I felt they had taken advantage of me despite the backbreaking work I did for them. Then, a new discomfort plagued me now that it was summer. It got very hot, so I took my shirt off while working in the fields. Picking up hay bales, my exposed inner arms became raw and red, and I was scratched and bruised all over my chest and stomach. I decided I had enough of the hard work and that family.

Through the efforts of my young friend Bernard, I got a new job with Francois Martin, a French farmer in the neighborhood. I shall never forget the first time I met him and his wife Madeleine. They were having dinner when I arrived, and my hungry eyes beheld the most delicious looking white potatoes, drenched in butter and mayonnaise. To this day, I adore little white potatoes with mayonnaise. In the care of the Martins, my food intake improved tremendously, and I gained back some of the weight I had lost. I was thankful to feel safe there and much happier.

My chores were mainly in the stables, taking care of the cows, horses and pigs. I didn't have to work in the fields; the only drawback of this job was that I had to sleep in the stable, which I did not mind. There was no space for a bedroom in their house. The stable was divided into three parts: the far end for the pigs, the middle for the cows and the near end for the horses.

Francois Martin told me to make myself comfortable near the end, with the horses. Between the horses and my "bedroom" was a six-meter-high red partition with a little door in the middle for me to go in and out. My sleeping quarters were primitive with a thick straw-filled mattress on the floor, but I liked sleeping there well enough. With the horses nearby, it was always nice, warm and cozy. But over time Esther refused to sleep in the barn with the animals, and our relationship somewhat deteriorated. In the end she decided to go back to the Suurds.

My peace at the new farm was soon shattered when the new ID Jan Suurd had secured for me rendered me visible to the bureaucrats. Since there was now an official record of me at the Prefecture of the Montreux Police, the German authorities were now aware of me. They needed able-bodied men as laborers and instructed the prefecture to issue orders to have all locals report for duty.

I didn't report because I had heard farm workers were exempt. It turned out the exemption didn't cover me because I was in a separate class from resident farmers. Soon a gendarme dressed in khaki and black, like the ones that had arrested me in Auxerre, arrived in the village and started asking for Pieter Lutgert. He went to the Suurds' house, where Esther told him I no longer worked there and she did not know my whereabouts.

Through rumors I found out young men of my age were to report to a certain location near Paris, to start filling bomb craters for the German Army. I didn't want anything to do with this. Filling bomb craters would not be so terrible, but I heard the Nazis would later take these workers to Germany, as forced labor. Even with my legitimate papers, the chances of survival there seemed minimal.

I had gotten to know an old man in the village, Charles Pitot, who had served in the First World War as a pilot – a job that greatly appealed to me. I had a great deal of respect for him and always called him Monsieur Pitot. I wanted his opinion, and I asked him what to do when the gendarmes were looking for me.

"Pierre don't let *les sales Boches* get hold of you," he advised. He knew someone who could help me, a gentleman farmer by the name of Alphonso Capelli. He was a rich Italian Fascist, who owned acres of woodland filled with rich timber and might be able to use me as a woodsman.

I asked him how I'd be better off with an Italian Fascist than with the nice French people I worked for now? He told me not to worry about Capelli, who was more interested in money than politics. The Germans needed lumber and his wood was the best source they had around here. If Capelli put me to work, Pitot assured me I would be protected because of his connections and privileges. He'd helped others and could probably help me too.

I went to see Alphonso Capelli on my own. He lived in a big house with vines climbing up the walls almost up to the roof's edge, surrounded by a well-manicured flower garden. When I rang the bell, a heavy-set woman opened the door and ushered me into a large vestibule. As I waited, I heard piano music coming from a room. I peeked through a connecting door and saw a pretty young girl playing a grand piano.

The girl noticed me, got up from the piano bench and gave me a warm smile. I asked her about Signor Capelli and she informed me that he was away on business and would not be back for a whole month. I didn't know her relation to my possible future boss, but being the young fellow that I was, I didn't mind getting into a conversation with her. Soon we were chatting like old friends. Among other things, I told her that, like her, I loved the piano classics: Chopin, Poulenc, Debussy and others.

As we talked, I sensed a spark of attraction between us, but another sense alerted me against getting too close. God knows who this girl might be, I thought. Was she the wife, daughter, or mistress of the Signor? Or maybe even a spy who could turn me over to the Germans? She was too much of a risk for me to get involved with. I said goodbye as politely as I could and went back to Pitot to seek further advice.

"Back again?" he asked, and not waiting for me to answer, he told me I had picked a good day to leave the village. Not one, but four gendarmes showed up with a truck and filled it with the young men they rounded up. They pasted a written order outside city hall for Pieter Lutgert and others to report to the Montreux prefecture immediately. I thanked him and told him I owed it to him that I still had my head on my shoulders. I had been extremely lucky because they were so interested in finding me that they went straight to the Suurd house and turned the place upside down despite the family's protestations that I no longer lived there. They certainly never thought to look for me at the house of a known Fascist and German collaborator.

I reasoned I'd better stay away from the village and hide out in the woods. Pitot agreed and wished he could help me. It was clear Pamfou was getting too hot for me. By that time, it was night. In the dark, I couldn't find any decent hiding places when I slipped into the forest. All I could find was a shallow indentation between two large trees. I could fit my entire body into the cavity, and I found some dead branches to cover my den. When morning came, I was surprised how well I had done in the dark. The branches over the depression were level with the forest floor all around.

I do not remember how many days I remained inside my hiding place. I do remember that I slept most of the time the first few days until hunger and thirst kept me awake. I felt dizzy and weak. I wandered around looking for something to eat when my eye caught what seemed like a long pin sticking out of the earth.

Clearing the brush I discovered to my great surprise that the pin was actually the end of a rusted bayonet still attached to the barrel of a rifle some First World War soldier had abandoned. There were more fragments and debris spread about the area. I spotted a small metal can half buried in the earth. Nearby there were two more hidden beneath dirt and foliage. Incredibly, they were not rusted and shaking them I heard that they contained a liquid. At least something to drink, I hoped.

The sharp end of a piece of a broken rifle barrel enabled me to pry open the top of one of the cans, and I could not believe my eyes when I found the tiniest, finely preserved gourmet mushrooms inside. It didn't take me long to finish off these delicacies, which greatly calmed my hungry stomach and made me feel much better.

For several weeks I had nothing to eat. I was constantly dizzy and the world around me appeared as a dream. I vividly remember I had set a trap on a rabbit's trail as Bernard had taught me to do. When I went back there later, I found a small rabbit caught in the snare. I released it and killed it. However, I can't recall eating it, most likely caused by my weakened and dizzy condition. Then one morning, I heard the clanging of chains, a man's voice yelling commands to a horse and a dog yelping on and off.

I worked my way cautiously toward the sounds and through the trees to spy on whoever caused the commotion. I saw a man and a powerful Friesian horse hauling felled trees. The clanging came from a heavy chain looped around the tree connected to the gear on the horse's back. I didn't approach the man right away but followed him at a distance. He worked skillfully, piling the logs along a ditch at the side of a road. I could see he had a lot of stamina. Working with logs, heavy chains and a horse required a lot of strength.

Toward midday, he stopped working and built a fire. From a small pack, he produced a black frying pan, a loaf of French bread, a slab of white lard and a number of eggs. At that, my stomach started doing a dance. I had not been truly in touch with the hunger I was experiencing. It seemed if you went hungry for a while, you really didn't feel it anymore. What I did feel was weakness in my arms and legs and dizziness when I moved my head too fast.

I didn't sense anything alarming about the woodsman and couldn't hold back from approaching him any longer. I stepped out of the woods and introduced myself. He said his name was Roland and he worked for Alphonso Capelli, the very same that Monsieur Pitot had referred me to earlier. For the rest, he said nothing – he silently continued preparing his lunch.

I followed his every move, transfixed, unable to take my eyes away from his large stash of food. He placed a piece of lard against his chest and began slicing it into thick slabs. Carefully, he removed the rind and threw it to the dog, which, without chewing, swallowed it whole.

Oh, how I envied that dog! My jealousy grew when the lard hit the hot frying pan. The sizzling of the fat and its delicious aroma spread all around me. I started salivating, my stomach crunching and aching. Roland then broke three or four eggs into the pan, placed the loaf of bread under his arm and started cutting it into thick slices. Again, the dog got the crust that fell off as he did the slicing.

I waited for him to offer some of the food, but it did not happen. He audibly swallowed his eggs, bacon and bread, occasionally throwing some to his dog. I didn't want to elicit any questions about why I was so hungry, so I just watched the scene, quietly and painfully suffering with a sharp, stabbing pain in my stomach.

I stayed there another few weeks, but I was so famished that I chanced sneaking into the village in the middle of the night to visit Pitot. He would ply me with as much food as I could keep down. He also kept me abreast of how the police were proceeding with tracking down the men they needed. Many of those who were targeted had also gone into hiding. After a while it seemed they had given up canvassing Pamfou and relative peace returned.

It was then that Pitot advised me to once again try to contact Alphonso Capelli, especially now that I had a good sense of the work he needed done. When I rang, the same heavy-set lady opened and again asked me to sit on a bench in their vestibule. This time Capelli was home, but I had to wait a long time before he made his entrance. He was a big and heavy-set man with a tanned face showing deep wrinkles. He had drooping bags under his eyes, and he wasn't pleasant to look at. His hair was disheveled and it looked as if he had just gotten out of bed after a night of heavy drinking. He wore tan riding breeches and a black shirt with the tail hanging out of his breeches.

I introduced myself as Pieter Lutgert. He responded in a deep, croaky voice asking about the purpose of my visit. A bit taken aback by his apparent inability to place me, I let him know it was Monsieur Pitot who told me to contact him.

"Who in Hell is Monsieur Pitot?" he demanded. A bit more desperate, I explained that he lived on Route Nationale in Pamfou and that they knew each other. Capelli scratched his head and rubbed his chin, obviously trying to recall the name. He seemed to have a flash of insight and asked if it was "that tall man who used to fly airplanes?" He finally got it right. I explained I had come here to ask him for a job working in the forest. Pitot had suggested he could use some help.

Capelli came to life and became more voluble. He said he indeed needed a hand, someone who could fell trees, strip them of their branches, saw them into meter-long logs, and pile them into *stères* (cubic meters). Was I up for the task?

I assured him I was. Suddenly, "I have been doing farm work all my life" came out of my mouth. When he asked me what kind of work, in my best French I lied like the dickens, giving him a story I thought would appeal to him. At the end, I added a bit of truth and said I also had worked as a farm hand for Jan Suurd. At the mention of this name, his eyes lit up and he agreed to give me the job. I do not recall what he offered to pay me, but I needed his protection more than his money. So, I became a woodsman.

It was very hard work, but I liked it. It exercised my muscles and kept me healthy. Lifting and handling the heavy logs without the luxury of gloves scraped the inside of my arms and hands, painfully at times, but there was nothing I could do about it. The weather was pleasant. Eventually I was able to go back and sleep in the barn at the Martins' farm; they were very easygoing. They let me come and go and do some work for them as well.

One day, I took time after work to visit Pitot, who gave me a big hello and asked if I still did work as a woodsman. I told him that I did and his advice had worked out just fine for me. It turned out it was a good thing for him too, he was running out of wood for his stove and fireplace and wanted me to collect some for him. I agreed to help, but asked how I would get the stuff back to Pamfou. He told me not to worry because he had a donkey and a cart that could handle the job. He took me to see that donkey housed in a little shed and introduced me to Babette.

I gave the donkey a weak smile, but she completely ignored me. I instinctively disliked her, and I really didn't know why. Maybe it was because I was more used to being around horses. Then Pitot took me to see the cart I was to use. It was open-ended on two large wheels, with two shafts in front to attach the donkey with a series of complicated straps. The whole contraption was made of wood and leather, with two wheels covered with a metal belt which made a clickety-clack noise rolling over cobblestone pavement. The two uprights on each side, as well as the one in front were high enough to allow a highly stacked cargo, leaving the rear open to facilitate loading.

I was to take Babette out to the spot in the forest where I worked, load the cart with small branches and firewood logs, and return whole load to him, for which he would pay me with butter, flour and a bit of money. Pitot described Babette as a docile animal when he noticed the wry face I was making at the donkey. He advised I should walk slightly in front of her, which would allow me to guide her gently with no problems. He strapped her to the shafts while murmuring softly and giving her small pats on the neck.

On the way to the woods, the procedure Pitot had suggested seemed to be working. I walked ahead of Babette, and she walked along gently. We stopped once we reached the area where I worked. Before I could finish tying her to a tree, she urinated, splashing some on me and shot me a look of contempt.

I cut some logs into a size that fit the cart and loaded them so they would keep the cart balanced. By the time I was done, the load was quite heavy. I loosened the reins from the tree, but when I tried to turn Babette around, she wouldn't let me. She did not want to move one inch. I pulled harder, shoved and pushed her, but that did not help.

I took a stick and hit her hard on the hind legs. That seemed to help. She shot forward, letting out an awful hee-haw, but after four steps, she came to a stop again. I tried to shove the cart while screaming at her, but we hardly moved a few feet.

At this point, I really lost my temper and gave the donkey a whack with all my might. When Babette felt the force of my anger, she suddenly bolted forward so forcefully, that it shifted the stacked lumber backwards. The jolt caused the front part of the cart to fly up, and poor Babette, who was strapped to the cart, was lifted upward along with it in one seesaw motion. She hung there in the air, braying, hissing and kicking with all four legs like a maniac. That additional motion caused the entire load to slide off the cart, shifting the weight and sending Babette crashing back to the ground.

All my work had been for nothing. The minute Babette's hooves hit the ground, she sprang forward, braying eerie hee-haws. She bolted to the road at full speed, the empty cart wildly swinging and swaying behind her. I ran after her, laughing and cursing at the same time. I moved as fast as my legs could go, but still I was unable to catch up with her. I gave up trying to catch Babette and hoped she would find her way home. When I finally reached Pitot's home, I found him standing there with a wide smile on his face and with Babette not far off. I described what had happened and we both burst out laughing.

PART III

JOINING THE RESISTANCE

CHAPTER 16

A Dried-Out Well

I WAS DEEPLY asleep in my bed in the stable back on the Martin farm when someone opened the barn door and woke me late one night. In the dark, all I could make out was the figure of a man with a cap on his head and I stiffened with panic. When I made out that it was Jean, the mayor of Pamfou who had regularly visited the Suurd farm, I was confused. He always gave me a polite nod whenever he saw me, but we had never exchanged conversation. My French was not so great back then, so I was often shy to speak with locals.

He was whispering something I tried to make sense of. I was still quite startled out of my sleep, and the intrusion put me on edge. I kept trying to understand what he was saying. I raised myself out of bed and as I got closer, "You English?" was all I could make out as he motioned me to follow him. So, I got dressed and went outside, still not comprehending what he wanted.

Was I in danger? My heart was racing. Was he going to turn me over to the police? A thousand thoughts went through my mind. I grabbed him by the lapels of his jacket and screamed in my poor French, "Where are you taking me? What's going on you bastard!" He sensed my fear and suspicion and immediately pointed his finger down several times whispering, "English...English." Then pointing to the sky, "English pilots."

Slowly I began to understand this was not an attempt to turn me over to the authorities. So, in the dead of night I followed him to the courtyard in front of his house. Here he put his finger to his lips.

"Shh… shh…" then again pointing downwards in rapid succession, "English pilots." He shushed me again. When I heard the word "pilots" repeatedly, excitement surged through me. Since my childhood, aviation and anything to do with flying had been part of a dream world that I fantasized being a part of.

He led me to a mound of hay in the center of his courtyard. Pushing aside several bales revealed a circular wooden cover on the ground. When he pushed it aside, it revealed the shards of broken bricks that once circled a water well. Looking down inside, it had obviously dried out, and the upper rungs of a ladder that stood on the bottom became partly visible. Moments later, a person rose from its depths. It was a man holding a lit lantern in his hand. He had a ruddy face, wore a cap and seemed to be wearing coveralls. The silence was broken when he asked me in a hushed British accent if I spoke English, and I nodded, my heart skipping a beat.

Moments later, a second person rose up the ladder. He was tall, with blond hair and a full beard. He spoke perfect French to the mayor, who motioned for the three of us to enter his house. My heart was pounding so loudly I could hear it in my ears, and a feeling of euphoria overwhelmed me; my breath was choking with excitement. Once inside we gathered around a table. The mayor's wife brought out a bottle of wine and we raised our glasses.

"*À la victoire!*" There was no doubt I was in good company.

The blond man with the beard introduced himself as Claude. He began in French, but when he realized I didn't understand everything, he switched to English. From listening to the radio, watching Hollywood movies, and what I learned at school, my English comprehension was not fluent, but good enough to understand what he was getting at. He would not react or answer my question when I asked if he was American, as I recognized his accent.

I figured out the ruddy-faced person who did not speak French at all, was a British RAF pilot who had been shot down. His name was Andrew and I couldn't take my eyes off him. I couldn't believe I had come face to face with a real pilot, a man who flew those wonderful machines that bombed the Germans.

Claude explained that they had established a very efficient network stretched across the German occupied zones. It's main purpose was to get Allied pilots that had been shot down back safely to their bases in England. The Germans had infiltrated and destroyed the main link of their underground resistance network, torturing members into betraying their friends and then executing them all. They were stranded hiding out in the well, without the ability to reestablish communication.

Claude and Andrew were both in hiding when the Germans conducted their raid and both managed to escape by the skin of their teeth. The Germans had Claude's description and Andrew's not being able to speak a word of French had resulted in stranding them here. Without the knowledge of the whereabouts of their surviving links to their network, they needed assistance. They asked me if I could help. I had been listening in awe.

"Of course I can help," the words shot out of my mouth before I could think about it.

Claude asked me if I was sure, because of the danger involved. My answer was straightforward: of course. I didn't care about the danger. I wanted to help in any way I could. I certainly didn't mind if Germans suffered in the process. I had nothing to hide amongst these men.

The next day gave me a chance to get down inside the well where they were hiding out. It was amazing. At the bottom, an opening led to a sizeable cave that could easily house three to four people. Wooden beams supported roof joists. The earthen floor was completely covered with mats of various sizes and colors. The arrangement seemed to date back to the First World War and probably had served as a secret cache for weapons. Here and there lanterns illuminated the entire area. There were two bedrolls on the floor that looked comfortable and cozy. In between stood a small three-legged stool.

When we had settled on the floor, the three of us immediately felt a sense of camaraderie. What bonded us was a united cause against the hated enemy forces. Claude outlined their problem further: they didn't have a transmitter and without one, they were hamstrung. He figured there might still be contacts alive in Paris, but he wasn't sure. He suggested I travel there to scout out some locations and reliable people. This mission had a degree of danger, but a start had to be made.

Again, Claude asked if I would still go and if I understood the danger. And again, I answered "yes" without hesitation. I actually looked forward to this adventure. So, he began preparing me and was very specific about how long I should stay in Paris. He gave me 48 hours, successful or not. I must be back before 8 p.m. He was sure to point out that if I was delayed or caught, he and Andrew would have to leave this place. The aim was to prevent anyone from tracing me back there.

When I arrived in Paris, I went to check on my trustworthy contacts at Hotel Belge, but neither Madame Gaston nor Michel were in. My other safe contact was the Van Houtte family. They were home and they couldn't believe it when I arrived unexpectedly. I did not dare mention the real reason for my visit to Paris. They thought I was insane to have left peaceful Pamfou and traveled to a dangerous Paris. Then finally, because I had no idea where or how to start my search for contacts, I revealed my discovery in Pamfou and they were delighted. Jules van Houtte immediately offered his contact at the Dutch Consulate.

I worried that all the officials the Germans had left in place at the Consulate were miserable Nazis, but Jules laughed and explained that, fortunately, the entire staff was fiercely anti-German – including the consul himself who had cleverly hidden his true feelings from the Germans. He warned me to be extremely careful and restrict my first inquiry to only one person, Mr. Van Loon. Jules had known him for many years and trusted him completely.

With that good news, I returned to Hotel Belge where I found Michel on duty. He looked tired and drawn, and his welcome was hardly cordial. When I asked him what was happening, he admitted he was worn out because his mother was in the hospital with pneumonia, and he had to run the place by himself. I told him I was sorry to hear about Madame Gaston and hoped her health improved. I didn't tell Michel the real purpose of my visit to Paris but I did ask him if he knew anyone who could repair my radio.

He couldn't think of anyone but would let me know if he did. He agreed to let me sleep in the basement of the hotel without charging me and let me know the police were no longer looking for me. It was damp in that little room, and I spent a restless night there, trying to sleep on the hard mattress on the floor. As early as I could, I slipped out of the hotel and made for the Dutch Consulate.

I followed Jules van Houtte's advice and asked for Mr. Van Loon. He was a tall gentleman with black wavy hair who greeted me with his hand stuck out. He led me to a small office and asked what he could do for me. We spoke in Dutch and I told him Jules van Houtte had suggested I seek out his help. He was elated and let it be known he would do anything against the Germans that he could.

I suggested I needed to get my hands on some form of communication, and he proposed a crystal radio. I wasn't up to speed on radio technology and didn't know what a crystal radio could do, but I thought it probably couldn't hurt. He believed his 16-year-old son, who had been tinkering with one, could be a starting point. I asked if I could get one when I returned in a couple of days, and he believed I could. Things were beginning to work out, which gave me the courage to ask if he could look around to see what else he could arrange for me in the meantime.

I took my leave from the Consulate and made sure to be back in Pamfou by eight o'clock, as Claude had instructed. He laughed when I told him that I could probably get someone to build a crystal radio.

"Good deal Pieter, well done," he said. Unfortunately, it turned out a crystal radio only received signals but couldn't send any. He was happy to get it anyway and thought if it was strong enough, we might be able to get some information from their base in England. I wanted to know the next steps, and he suggested I wait two days and go back and see what my contact had been able to arrange.

Claude was a quiet person; he did not speak much and mostly nodded in response. His voice was calm and amazingly, he spoke French without an accent, even though his English had a distinct American twang. I tried to get him to tell me more about himself but he ignored my questions. Two days later, I returned to the Dutch Consulate and Tim van Loon handed me a small tin can. He was proud of what his son had made in just one day. When I opened the can, there, ingeniously concealed, was a crystal radio. This was good, but when I asked if he had anything else for me, he replied, "Not yet."

I was happy to return to Pamfou with my first mission accomplished and when I handed the crystal radio to Claude, a smile came to his face, but he did not say anything.

CHAPTER 17

Transitions and Transmissions

THE NEXT TIME I was in contact with Claude, he ordered me back to Paris and suggested I look up a print shop on Rue Scribe, not far from the Place de l'Opéra. He had information that an underground group had been printing anti-German pamphlets there. If it was safe to enter, I was to look for a man by the name of Melo and hand over a parcel; this contact might have names and locations that could be helpful.

I agreed to the plan. Claude cautioned me not to be too impetuous; I needed to be extra vigilant. Pamphlet distribution was a risky business and the shop might be under surveillance. Again, I agreed, but he warned me against being so agreeable. Claude had become impatient. He needed me to understand that under no circumstances was I to enter that shop without making sure it was safe. I was to pass by it several times and observe it from a distance. He could not afford me getting caught and wanted me back within 24 hours, again, no later than 8 p.m. He reminded me that if I arrived one minute later, I would not find them here. He wanted to be certain I understood the details.

To make absolutely sure, he warned me that if I sensed I was being followed, to not turn my head to look back. I had to enter a store or turn into a side street and then hide if possible. I nodded, but he wasn't done. If I was hiding, I had to check someone had indeed been following me. If I recognized the same face twice or more, I could be sure I was being followed. I indicated I understood, but he still wasn't convinced. He wanted me to be mindful that there could be two, or even three, different people tailing me. Agents alternated positions, so it might not be the same person each time. The best way to shake a tail was to enter a place with a rear exit, because they would be expecting me to come out the front door, but I would've made my escape out the back.

With all these words of warning in my head, I again boarded the bus to Paris with the small parcel hidden inside a baguette in my metal lunchbox. I spotted the print shop on Rue Scribe without difficulty. I scrutinized it from the opposite side of the street. From there, I couldn't detect anything out of the ordinary. I then made several passes in front of it and noticed the place was locked, with no light was on inside. I spotted the police seal on the door, which told me plenty. I got out of the area as fast as possible.

I traveled back and forth from Pamfou to Paris for a period of about a month, delivering messages written on small pieces of folded up paper. I had to hide them in three different public urinals that Claude specified. I would slide them behind the water tank and never knew what the messages said. I also never knew the people who picked up the messages.

I often carried these secret messages between two thick slices of baguette inside a brown satchel many French workers used to carry their lunch. On two occasions, I survived a check by French police. It was completely nerve-racking, but my official *laissez-passer* ID and ideal hiding spot let me pass me without any problems.

A few times I had to knock on doors and deliver parcels. I suspect they were to help reestablish the underground resistance network that had been destroyed. Sometimes I would also be a target spotter, pointing out railroad tracks or specific buildings that needed to be bombed. I followed Claude's instructions for what to look for, but I was never involved in any violence.

I was also carefully feeling out people for a radio transmitter without any real success. On my own, I decided to return to the Dutch Consulate one day. Tim greeted me with wide-open eyes, happy to see me since he had no way to get in touch with me. He said he had great news. His son's teacher, a trustworthy person, said he could convert an ordinary radio into a transmitter for me. In fact, by now it should be fully assembled. This was an excellent turn of events. However, I let him know that even if it were ready now, I couldn't risk taking it back with me. A transfer like that would need lots of planning.

I returned to Pamfou and shared the good news. Claude wasn't normally a man to waste words on praise, but this time his face lit up and he said I had handled this in just the right way. If we succeeded in getting a working transmitter, it would greatly improve their situation. However, we needed to be extra cautious about smuggling it here. We would all be in grave jeopardy if caught.

I could not fall asleep that night. I was happy Claude had given me a compliment, and I kept thinking about the risk involved in transporting the transmitter. During my bus trips to Paris so far, I had encountered no contraband searches or ID checks by police, except for my return trip to Pamfou when I experienced a close call. Just before I got to the bus terminal, I spotted helmeted German police in the trucks they used for raids, speeding into the plaza. They dismounted while their officers screamed orders and surrounded the entire plaza. Fortunately, I was still just outside the perimeter. Had I arrived a few minutes earlier, I would have been inside the trap. And now I wasn't sure how I was going to go through that same plaza with a radio transmitter.

A new member had joined our group: André, who had taken my job at Francois Martin's farm after I started working for Claude. He was a friend of Bernard. I liked André and was glad he was on board. He was in his late twenties, with a heavy black tuft of hair constantly obstructing his vision, which didn't seem to bother him. Recently he had become a father. Claude decided to let André and Jean, the mayor of Pamfou, travel to Paris with me to help arrange the safest way to fetch the radio transmitter.

To carry such a dangerous item from the Consulate on Boulevard Haussmann to the nearest Metro station came with its own set of dangers. The very idea of entering a subway train with it gave me the chills. Police and spies in civilian clothes would often be on board checking IDs and examine passengers' suitcases and parcels. If I were caught carrying a radio transmitter, it would mean tortuous interrogation and certain death by the Gestapo.

We decided to transfer the transmitter in stages. The first stage would be moving it from the Consulate to the Metro, and the discussion centered around how best to do it. I suggested walking it over while in disguise. I told them my previous ploy of dressing as a woman met with great success. I could hide the transmitter under my dress, using padding to make me look fat all over and hide the transmitter.

André suggested we try it out, so we took a cooking pot about the size of the transmitter and tried putting it under my clothes after I dressed in the mayor's wife's clothes. It didn't work; André could see it the minute I moved. He got an idea in the process. He asked us if we noticed how bakers in Paris delivered their bread by placing the baked goods in a basket inside a wooden box mounted on the front of a tricycle. We all liked the idea. We would try to secure a tricycle and hide the transmitter under a pile of bread sticks in the basket.

To reduce the risk, we'd keep the stages of movement short – about the distance of a normal bakery delivery. That required three different safe houses on the way to the bus station. Our covert operation would work best with the least number of people involved. However, we realized that to carry out the breadbasket scheme in several stages, we needed the extra help. Jean, the mayor, said he probably could find two or three willing and trustworthy helpers in the village.

They wanted me to find the three safe houses in Paris and a baker's tricycle, but I declined, reasoning it would be less conspicuous if a local resident or a French person did that job. Tim, my contact, found a trusted French employee of the Consulate, and both had everything lined up in a relatively short period of time. We agreed to strictly limit the number of people who knew the location of the safe houses. Even within our own circle, we told people no more than they needed to know for their own part of the operation. When Jean recruited the two helpers that he found in Pamfou, we didn't even reveal the presence of Claude and Andrew to them.

When I made my next trip to Paris and back to Pamfou, I got an indication of how risky our plan was, even with the extra help. Nearing the bus terminal, I saw plainclothes policemen inspecting all travelers carrying parcels or suitcases. It made me nervous, but since I wasn't carrying anything, they did not even look at me. I got on the bus safely but shaken. Even so, we proceeded with the operation; all parts were in place and Claude needed us to proceed so he could reestablish his resistance network. Our group consisted of Mayor Jean, André, the two new helpers and me. The five of us took the bus to Paris together and we seated ourselves separately.

As it turned out the transmitter wasn't at the Consulate at all. It had remained with the man who had put it together and his son agreed to bring it to a trusted bakery near his house just before the store closed. The operation ran to the minute. Precisely at 11 a.m. the next morning, the unit was placed inside the wooden box on the baker's tricycle, hidden underneath a pile of bread sticks. One of the helpers from Pamfou pedaled to the first safe house by 11:40 a.m. André took it to the second safe house by 12:50 p.m. I had been following the entire operation on a regular bike, making sure everything went smoothly.

At 1 p.m., the second helper from Pamfou took the unit to the third house. He arrived at 1:25 p.m., also without incident. We had planned to catch the last bus of the day at 4 p.m., so we had two hours to wait out. André and Jean met us at safe house number three and decided to stake out the bus terminal during that extra time. Meanwhile, I was sitting on pins and needles, because I was the one who had been selected for the most dangerous leg of the trip – taking the transmitter from the last safe house to the bus terminal. The second helper would be trailing me on the regular bike.

At 3:30 p.m., I donned a white baker's apron and started pedaling. I had a bad sense of direction, and I worried whether I was taking the correct boulevards and streets. My helper was a great support. He moved faster than me; sometimes he rode ahead to look for trouble and lead me in the right direction. Other times, he rode behind as a tail, to make sure I wasn't being followed. When he was out of sight, I worried the most.

As we came closer, I was wet with perspiration. I should have been calmer, because we had planned so well. I hadn't made a single wrong turn, and finally the terminal came into sight. Now came the really tricky job, getting the thing onto the bus. I spotted Jean. He had a broad smile and nodded to me. He had not detected any danger. We'd all agreed that the signal would be that if he tied his shoes, it meant I should turn back, but fortunately all was well. André was posted near our bus, also with a smile. The coast was clear. I handed off the tricycle to André, and got into the bus, with the transmitter at the bottom of a bag of baguettes. The bus took us to Pamfou without incident, and when I arrived at the mayor's yard, Claude proudly took possession of the transmitter. To my surprise, this quiet man let out a loud "Yippee!" and slapped me on the back in utter joy.

Claude explained we would have to wait to use the transmitter and would have to use it sparingly, to not risk exposing our hiding spot. There were listening devices that could detect our signal, and we'd come this far not to be foolish. As soon as the transmitter came online, he quickly reestablished contact with his home base in England. To me, the dots and dashes of their codes were incomprehensible, but I still found it exciting to listen in. It gave me a feeling of safety, because freedom existed where those sounds came from. I was elated that the mission was a success, but soon my job as a courier expanded. Claude could not risk leaving his hiding place in the dry well, since there was no indication the Germans had stopped looking for him.

After having been accused of being a spy back in Auxerre, I had actually become one.

CHAPTER 18

SS Raid

THE FLOW OF information began to increase. The network was steadily being repaired and started to become effective again. My efforts were paying off. One night an armed resistance worker I didn't know came by to pick up Andrew. The network chain had been reestablished to the point where they were able to get him back to England. Of course, Claude remained as he was the kingpin of the network.

He was always reserved and used his words sparingly. I never heard him raise his voice. I began to realize Claude became more or less a father figure to me. I had the feeling he cared about me and worried about my safety during the many missions I completed for him. At one point, I found out to my surprise that he did not tell me everything that was going on. My ego felt injured at first, but as time passed, I realized this was the way the game had to be played. The less I knew, the less I would reveal under pressure or torture; it was safer for me, and for everyone this way.

This point was brought home horribly one day when André's young wife suddenly appeared with her baby in her arms, screaming and sobbing. André's body had been discovered in a nearby field – he had been shot through the head. Apparently, he was involved in a sabotage I hadn't known about, and he had been caught by the Germans.

It was at that horrid, sad moment I realized that Claude was selecting me for the less risky tasks and sending others to do the actual dangerous missions, like the kind that claimed André's life. Things like planting explosives, raiding enemy installations and undertaking other covert activities. The only thing Claude said to me when I asked him about that was, "André now belongs to the righteous French heroes." That was all that he would say about André's death.

Of course, all our activities boded danger for us. And then one day, neighboring farmers who were aiding us reported that a sizeable SS company was seen moving towards our neighborhood. They were likely linked to the group that had captured and executed André.

We assumed these SS soldiers might also be hunting for Claude, and he immediately ceased operating our transmitter. The Germans had new radio detection equipment, and sending or receiving signals would be a dead giveaway of our location. We were undecided about what to do. One possibility was that the searchers were only going to generally sweep the area; the other was that they might have an idea where Claude was hiding. In the first case, Claude might just as well stay where he was; the well was an unusually good hiding place. If they were going to do an especially thorough search of the mayor's place, however, it might be better to move Claude elsewhere.

We gathered in the mayor's kitchen to find solutions. Our cell now consisted of five operatives: Claude, Jean, two middle-aged men from the resistance who had just arrived and I. We reviewed the layout of Pamfou. Even the mayor, who knew the place inside out, couldn't pinpoint any place in town that would offer a better hiding place.

Jean pointed out most homes had cellars and attics, but those would pose no challenge for the SS. Even if Claude was to hide in one of those, they could easily catch him with their sniffing dogs and stethoscopes. Also, Claude did not want to risk exposing any more villagers to danger by asking for their help. I told them about my hiding spot in the forest. It had worked at the time, but I'd have been a dead duck if search dogs were involved.

One of the new men asked about some other town around here wondering if it would be any safer. Claude didn't think so as travel itself wasn't safe for a person on the SS hot list, plus there were too many informants and spies around. In the end, we all agreed that moving Claude anywhere else would be more dangerous than keeping him here; the hiding place in the well was ingeniously designed with its cave at the bottom of the pit.

We did decide we should make the mayor's yard more challenging for searchers. So far, the wellhead had been hidden with bales of hay. However, a pile of hay might suggest to searchers something or someone was hidden inside or underneath. So, we decided to make the bales a decoy, and stacked them prominently near a work shed.

Following the same reasoning, Claude suggested that rather than hiding the well's opening, we should make it more conspicuous and innocent looking. If they had to remove the cover to look inside, they wouldn't see anything but an empty shaft, so they would leave and look elsewhere.

"But what will we do about the ladder?" someone said.

That question about the ladder bedeviled us for a while. The well was too deep and the ladder too long to hide inside the cave. Stashing the ladder elsewhere might arouse suspicion. It also would isolate Claude in the event he needed to get out. Jean suggested sawing the ladder in half and hinging it. However, when we measured it, the halves were still too long to fit into the cave. Jean then suggested taking the ladder apart and using the rungs to make a rope ladder, which could be rolled up and put into the cave. We asked all our friends in the village, but nobody had rope long and strong enough. Jean decided we could use bed sheets instead. When he broached the idea with his wife, her face dropped, but Jean persisted.

He twisted and knotted the sheets around the ladder's rungs. The result looked funny, but the rungs held and fit nicely inside the cave. However, this solution posed another problem. The top of the rope ladder would have to be suspended from hooks at the rim of the well. If Claude had to get out, he would be unable to hang the ladder up. And we on the outside had no way to raise it from the bottom. We tried many contraptions to elevate the rope ladder, but none of them worked. Meanwhile, time was running out and tempers flared.

The best solution, we finally realized, was for Claude to stay where he was until we came for him. We developed a signal for him: three short raps and two scrapes on the wooden cover of the well. Then Claude could bring the rope ladder out of the cave and we'd haul it up with hooks on a long rope. We cleaned Jean's wife out of more sheets and knotted them to make the rope. In case Claude had to stay hidden for long periods, we lowered an empty pail for a toilet.

To camouflage the cave itself, we hung a dark-colored curtain at the bottom of the well, covering the entrance. Even without it, the cave opening was difficult to detect, but with the curtain, it became virtually invisible. We still had one major worry: would sniffer dogs be able to detect Claude hiding inside his hollow cave at the bottom of the 12-foot well? Some of us thought this might be possible; others said, "impossible." It did not matter. We couldn't think of a way to shield Claude further. We just had to hope and pray for the best and to do what we could to calm our nerves. We were on edge, especially when we kept hearing that the German search party was still combing the neighborhood and coming closer.

We rehearsed a scenario of what a search party would find around the mayor's place. Coming into the yard, they would see a work shed on the right and next to it, a pile of hay bales. On the left, they would find a small stable and henhouse. In the center of the yard, they would see the remnants of an abandoned water well, with most of the stones and brickwork that once surrounded its opening gone. They would see a wooden lid over the opening, held down with a rock, ostensibly to protect people from falling in.

We stationed some friends in the fields beside the roads leading from the mayor's place to Pamfou so they could give us advance warning. I was sleeping in my makeshift room in the stable and it was about three o'clock in the morning when yelling outside and the alarmed mooing of the cows suddenly woke me. I was disoriented and my heartbeat went into overdrive. This must be the raid we were expecting.

Immediately, I worried about Claude. Did someone alert him? Did he know? I didn't dare go outside to see. I heard the search party getting closer by their banging on walls and dogs barking. I heard their jackboots clanging on the pavement outside before they flung open the door to the partition behind which I slept.

"Papers!" one of the goons screamed at me. There were two of them, both SS officers. Their faces resembled steel masks that seemed to be of one piece with their frightening steel helmets. They looked like robots, inhuman. Shaking all over, I fumbled among my meager possessions to find my *laissez-passer*. As I held it out, one of the pair ripped it from my trembling hands and demanded to know my name.

"Pieter Lutgert," came out of my throat, in a voice I did not recognize. I was thankful I had been using my fake name long enough that it became second nature. The steel mask bent down, quickly scanning the document, and then flung it back at me. The two stiffly turned around and were gone. Oh God, what a relief! The barn I slept in had always been pleasantly warm from the heat the animals gave off, but now it had become so hot and oppressive, I couldn't breathe. I felt as if I were going to vomit. My heart was beating so fast it made me even more scared. I distinctly remember thinking I was going to have a heart attack. To get some air, I ran outside despite my fear and I found myself facing what looked like the entire German army.

The scene was surreal and difficult to explain. As I exited the barn, I saw rows of soldiers standing at attention in the yard, with three goons apparently at the head of command. Even in that remote farmyard, the SS operatives were totally focused on rank and protocol. Goon 1, who seemed to be the commander, screamed something to Goon 2 who passed on the command to Goon 3. He turned to me and screamed something in French (with a heavy German accent), asking me where I lived. I pointed at the barn for my answer. Apparently, Goon 3 understood my gesture. He passed a report of it up the line via Goon 2 to Goon 1 in command. This kind of indirect communication went back and forth a second time, until finally Goon 3 yelled out, "Get out of here immediately! You're in a military zone. Move fast or we'll shoot."

I didn't have to be told twice, and I blindly ran away from this terrifying scene. I raced past the stable, unable to go back inside. There were upwards of 50 soldiers all standing at attention. I passed a number of army trucks and smaller vehicles stationed around the place. Soldiers were milling around and a few were stretched out on the grass further out. As I continued, one of the soldiers muttered in French, "We treated you French too well."

I stopped running and took a look at the soldiers lounging near the farmyard. They seemed friendlier than the SS men I had just run away from. Apparently, the group who yelled at each other and me in the yard were unvarnished SS, while the soldiers around the farm belonged to the Wehrmacht. These ordinary soldiers didn't act hostile at all. One of them, a gray-haired, middle-aged man, began a conversation with me in French. He had a kind face and gave me a piece of black bread. It tasted horribly sour but eating it helped calm me down.

My French was as bad as his, but that didn't seem to register. He took me for a local farm boy like the others had, back at the barn. In the back of my mind gnawed the question of how well our hiding place was holding out. Under the circumstances, it would be insane to go near the well to find out. I would have to wait and exercise my patience.

The SS finally left after staking out the farm for three days. I went back to my old job on the Martin farm, replacing my friend Bernard, who was needed for other activities. During the raid, the Martins' home and farm were ransacked, as were several other innocent residences in the village. I had kept on working for Francois Martin off and on when I had been doing my underground work. He never raised his eyebrows or asked questions about my many lengthy absences. I am sure he had an idea of my involvement with the resistance, especially after the execution of André.

I purposefully stopped contacting Claude and Jean and stayed low for about three weeks. I certainly wanted to see them, but I still feared repercussions from the search. Late one night Jean appeared next to my bed in the barn as he had done that first night. Before I was even half-awake, he whispered in my ear just three short words: "Claude needs you!"

Silently we walked to his house. On entering the kitchen, I saw Claude emerging from one of the cupboards, his usual hiding place when not in the well. We shook hands and slapped each other on the back, thankful we survived the ordeal. I asked how he had coped during the three-day German raid.

I listened to what had occurred at the mayor's place. They locked Jean in a room for three days and interrogated him without letup. They questioned him more as the Mayor of Pamfou than as a suspected member of the underground. Nonetheless, they turned his home upside-down and they tore apart everything standing in the yard, including the haystack. The worst part was the moment the searchers pushed aside the well cover, but their search dogs ignored it.

They even sent a beam from a strong searchlight down the shaft, but they didn't spot the cave that was recessed from the bottom and camouflaged by the dark curtain. Thank God, Claude had stayed safe. Claude feared the worst and had a small container of cyanide that he had never told me about standing by. He'd rather have ended his life than be captured. Thankfully, he heard the searchers move away. He counted each step of their hobnailed jackboots as they faded into the night. Smugly and excitedly, we recounted all the ways in which we had prepared and been successful in hoodwinking the Germans.

Although Claude wanted to use our radio transmitter to tell our contacts in England we were safe, we had to keep radio silence. He reminded us the Germans sometimes left listening devices or spies behind to pick up radio signals. Much later, we finally dared to transmit a very brief "All okay" signal and held our breath, but nothing untoward happened. Still, Claude was cautious and held back on any more radio contact or underground activities. In fact, we hardly talked. Somehow, the silence made us feel safer.

Then, like a clap of thunder, Claude turned to me and announced, "I've been ordered back to England."

PART IV

FIGHTING BACK

CHAPTER 19

From Hell to Heaven

CLAUDE WAS LEAVING. I couldn't believe what he just said. I didn't want it to be true. A feeling of emptiness entered my whole being as I envisioned life without him. He had given me a sense of purpose and hope. When he had my attention again, he explained he was to proceed to a specific location at a certain date and time, at which point an airplane would secretly land and pick him up.

The planned rendezvous was in the Champagne district, approximately 200 kilometers away. This region had vast open spaces between small, scattered villages. It was a good choice for landing, but once more, it presented the risk of moving Claude away from the hiding place that had proved so successful. Intense radio traffic ensued to coordinate the many legs of his journey. When the time came to say goodbye, I was prepared to return to my work on the farm. But to my great surprise, he told me, "Get yourself ready." I was to travel with him to the rendezvous point.

Even though it was fraught with danger, I was excited at the chance to be on one more mission – and this time with Claude. On the designated evening at twilight, a strange-looking truck pulled into the mayor's yard and four armed men jumped out. They motioned for Claude and me to get in, and after emotional goodbyes between Jean and Claude, we started a two-hour trip to a farm where six more armed men greeted us. They led us into a barn where a table with bread and wine awaited. We filled our bellies with a late supper and then crawled into a big pile of hay for the night.

I could not find sleep. Despite the coziness of my resting place, my nerves were on edge. Memories of being on the run and hunted by Germans kept prying themselves into my awareness. I found some comfort in the fact that the men who guarded us were armed with pistols and three Mauser machine guns captured from the Germans. Yet, I knew we were no match for an armed force like the one that had raided the mayor's place. Chances of escape from a raid were not only slim; they were practically impossible.

I also worried about the airplane that was to pick Claude up. I could not imagine how an airplane could land without the Germans noticing. In my imagination, I saw hundreds of Germans surrounding the plane and killing us all. In the early morning hours of my restless night, I noticed a small kitten sitting on a ledge not far from me. It had a cute little face and kept blinking its eyes each time I called out to it. It wouldn't come to me, so I crawled to it. It let me pick it up, and I held its soft, furry body next to me for comfort. As we cuddled in the hay, I finally fell asleep. I also rested during the next day because we stayed on that farm until the next nightfall.

We took it slow on our way to the rendezvous, and the whole trip took about two weeks. During daylight, we stayed hidden, usually in barns on isolated farms. Even though additional men we picked up along the way expanded our armed party to 25, we didn't encounter a single challenge and never saw a single German. It helped that we stayed away from populated areas.

When we finally arrived near the landing place, we couldn't find hiding places for 25 people and a truck. The organizers hadn't given proper thought to this detail. In this isolated spot, there were no villages, huts nor farmyards with haystacks to hide in. The best we could do was camouflage ourselves with tall grass stems, brushwood, twigs and debris. It was difficult to cover the truck properly, but we did our best. We lay down in grass fields and waited there until darkness set in.

At dusk, most of the armed men said goodbye and drove away in the truck. I was proud to be part of such a major operation. I knew the network we had helped rebuild now functioned successfully. Two armed fighters stayed behind with Claude and me. I didn't know why the others left and I stayed. I felt uneasy lying there unprotected in an open field. We waited for days, with little to do. We had enough food but little to drink. I began to doubt the operation would succeed, and I voiced my concern to Claude. He also looked worried but, typical of him, he said little to calm my worries, except, "We're lucky that it hasn't rained yet!"

One evening, near twilight, a small single-engine monoplane appeared over the horizon. In the far distance, her engine gave off a soft, deep purr, much like the kitten I had slept with on our way. But as the plane circled downward, the purr became an ear-piercing roar. Transfixed, I saw the plane descend until her wheels touched the ground. This was really happening; I was mesmerized.

It was the first time I had ever seen an airplane land, although I had seen many planes in my dreams. Airplanes belonged to another world for me. I once visited a small airplane museum in my old hometown of Rotterdam, and I had marveled at the exhibits on display there. When I touched an airplane rudder on display at the time, I jumped for joy. It was a wonderful feeling that always stayed with me.

The plane came to a stop some distance away, then taxied toward us with its engine still roaring at high speed. Claude started to run towards it, beckoning me to bring a parcel I had been carrying for him. He had his hands full with two leather pouches. Breathlessly I followed. I stumbled and almost dropped the parcel, and now I was right beside the airplane. Claude crawled into her bulging belly, the propeller wash almost blowing me away as I went to hand the parcel up to him. He grabbed it, tossed it in and then both his hands shot out, hooked under my shoulders, and to my astonishment – he pulled me inside the plane.

It's impossible for me to find words to describe the feeling that overcame me at that moment. In a way, my mind went blank. In another way, my feelings turned to fright as the pilot revved up the engine. I felt the plane lifting into the air and the tug of gravity as we gained elevation. This was the first time I had ever flown in an airplane. I had dreamed so often about flying and now I was actually doing it.

When Claude pulled me inside, I landed face-down on the floor, and I stayed there a while. For the first time, I had no words. I took in the smell of gasoline fumes as if they were fragrant perfume. I felt the vibrations spreading through the plane's body, and I swayed as the plane banked, making its turns. Then it made a dip so tight that one wing pointed straight to the ground, which terrified me. I believed we were going to crash; after all my escapes, I would end up dead. I kept reacting to the motion of the plane and as much as I liked the idea of flying, the fear of crashing was overwhelming.

CHAPTER 20

England and Beyond

I WAS COMPLETELY disoriented when the plane landed in England, and I felt dizzy. It was as if I had no feet – I was floating. A cacophony of noises surrounded me: voices shouting and engines roaring. There were uniforms all around me. I had no idea where we had landed. Claude had disappeared. My mind was unable to assess my situation; I was too confused and still in shock.

I was outside in the darkness, so I moved to a nearby building. I stumbled into a brightly lit hall, and the contrast blinded and dazed me. When my eyes adjusted, I saw uniformed men milling around or sitting behind desks. I had trouble realizing they were not like the Germans I had so recently been confronted with. I was out of words when two uniformed men began to question me in English. Apparently, Claude hadn't told anyone he had brought along an extra passenger. They were asking me, "What is your name? Where were you born? Where do you live? Where did you come from?"

Automatically, I produced my French *laissez-passer*, which was crumpled and wet. It instilled no confidence. I think they believed I was a spy. I was used to being Pieter Lutgert, a documented French farm worker – certainly not a Jewish boy on the run. It took me a while to get used to the fact I had landed on a British airfield, and that British Field Security officers were the ones interrogating me.

When I regained some of my senses, I started making more sense to them. Soon they understood I was no spy, and because I said I was from

Rotterdam, they sent me to a nearby Dutch military camp. At the time of the German invasion of Holland, the Dutch army was overwhelmed, but some military units escaped to England and formed the so-called Princess Irene Brigade. The Queen and the Dutch government also fled and set up a government in exile. After I arrived at the Dutch brigade, I finally realized I was in good hands. After an eternity of hiding my real identity, I revealed my real name to the Dutch officers and told them I was a Jew who had escaped from the Germans.

Since I had first-hand knowledge about how things stood across the Channel, they questioned me kindly for several days. They wanted to know the names of Dutch collaborators and spies, locations, and events, and I gave them as much information as I had. Unfortunately, I could not give them the name of the traitor who had awoken me with a gun to my head in my own family's apartment. Nor did I know the identity of the other Dutch traitor, who had arrested me on a streetcar in Amsterdam and whom I had left disabled and holding my overcoat.

The Dutch brigade gave me a box containing a razor and other toiletries. It also contained a letter, signed by Queen Wilhelmina, welcoming me to "this Island of Freedom." They expected me, as a Dutch citizen, to join the Dutch brigade, but I didn't want to. What I wanted was to go to America and become a fighter pilot. The Dutch promised I could get pilot training with the British Royal Air Force if I joined the Dutch army. Nevertheless, I did not commit. I still felt as if I were in a dream and didn't know where to go or what to do.

Days later, I was in the middle of being questioned by Dutch Intelligence officers, when I saw an American man in uniform approach. I couldn't believe my eyes; I recognized the man was Claude, clean-shaven and in a full U.S. military officer's uniform. It had taken him some searching in the Dutch chain of command to track me down. We hugged and backslapped each other like we used to do at the mayor's place in France. He told me I could still call him Claude, except that around the military, I should say Captain Claude like everyone else.

He never revealed his surname, but much later, someone told me that his name wasn't Claude at all; they said his full name was Henry Miller. Whether that is factual, I never found out. Until then, of course, he didn't know my real name either, and he laughed when I told him my last name.

"Okey dokey, Boeki," he chuckled. Claude told the Dutch brigade officers I was working with him, and that they had no authority over me. I was under the auspices of the American government, Office of Strategic Services, or OSS. They had no choice but to release me.

He showed up with a set of U.S. Army fatigues and a pair of brown para-boots. I wasted no time changing into the gear, which surprisingly fit me well. Up until then, I was still dressed in the crumpled clothing I wore back in France, with the boots Bernard had given me in Pamfou. A change came over me. I felt my chest swelling as the new fatigues and boots transformed me into an American soldier. Technically, I was still a civilian, but now I felt like part of the thousands of American soldiers around me.

One of the few things I shall never forget was the food the Americans served. In France, I had to subsist on meager food and sometimes went hungry altogether. You can imagine how I felt when I first saw and tasted real U.S. army bread. The square slice was pure white and did it ever taste delicious. Then someone handed me a hamburger, round and thick, with cooking oil dripping from it. I folded another slice of white bread around it, and the taste will remain in my mouth forever.

It felt good to sense the enormous might and power I lived in the middle of: gigantic bulldozers, cannons, tanks, trucks and jeeps (the first I had ever seen). War material of all kinds neatly lined up, ready for action, as far as the eye could see. These olive-drab instruments of war radiated an energy I could feel. I felt as if I were a part of an unstoppable juggernaut and I, an invincible combatant.

Claude arranged for me to get aboard a ship to the United States. He handed me a sealed envelope to give to the immigration officials at the U.S. port of entry, but he didn't tell me where that would be. We said goodbye.

The ship was named the USS *Primrose* or some other flower-sounding name. Again, the cuisine I remember the best, specifically the taste and color of the coffee that was served on board.

I needed to know how everything mechanical worked, so I had a close look at the engine room and the ship's controls. I also spent a great deal of time in the wheelhouse, where, to my surprise, the helmsman showed me we were zigzagging. I was totally unaware danger lurked beneath the waters in the form of U-boats. After a week or so we reached Boston.

Two tall men dressed in civilian clothes and wide-brimmed hats picked me up from the dock. I handed them the large, sealed envelope Claude had prepared for me. They took me to be questioned once again by a new set of officials, including two stubborn bullies who apparently took a strong dislike to me. Thanks to them, I spent my first night in the U.S. in custody, locked up in a windowless room. In the morning, I insisted on seeing the supervisor of the immigration office and mentioned Claude, which seemed to help. I was told to wait.

Of course, I didn't have anywhere to go, so I had nothing to do but wait. Two tall men dressed in civilian clothes and wide-brimmed hats picked me up. I had no idea what organization they belonged to. I hadn't had any breakfast, so they took me to a diner, where I ate my first stack of American pancakes. The coffee did not taste as good as what they had served on board the ship. Everything was unfamiliar, and for days I followed people blindly. I was bewildered and dazed, living in an unreal world as they took me on endless train trips to places I did not know, or had ever heard of. It made my head spin.

Finally, I was taken to a camp where I was sworn into duty in the United States Armed Forces. Whenever I was able to find someone with authority, I asked in a huff why they hadn't sent me to pilot training, which is what I really wanted. They put me off, saying it might happen later. They said it was important for me to get counterintelligence training first.

I was given an access pass with a number on it marked "Camp Ritchie," which is how I learned the name of where I was. Apparently, the army officials had been told of my background, and they gave me an orientation. Afterwards, I began my training in counterespionage. By this time, I understood that in the military, they said one thing and did another. Soon I found myself in basic training in Fort Benning, Georgia. I remember the heat and humidity and how the discomfort kept me awake at night. I recall long treks with full gear on my back. I can still feel the weight of the steel helmet on my head.

After this ordeal was over, I knew how to handle an M1 rifle, carbine, tommy gun and a .45-caliber pistol. Days and weeks of shooting practice on the rifle range left a constant ringing in my left ear. The result of which, years later, I lost half of my hearing capacity in that ear. They also spent untold hours drilling my army serial number into my brain, but I have forgotten it since.

In a rare free moment during my basic training. I was lounging outside the barracks, when an officer strode up. I saluted as I was trained; he saluted back and in a gruff voice ordered me to drive. He pointed me to get in a nearby jeep. I had never even driven a car before, let alone a jeep with its many gears, but clearly this man would not take any form of insubordination. I wouldn't have dared to say no to a superior, so I shyly said, "Yes sir," and climbed into the jeep.

I had watched others drive, so I knew to turn the key to start the jeep, and I remembered to push the clutch pedal down. I shifted into low gear – it was marked – but I had neglected to release the clutch slowly. I let it pop up. The jeep lurched forward, almost throwing the officer in the back seat onto the street.

"Don't you know how to drive, soldier?" he snarled at me as he climbed back into the vehicle. I was too busy trying to control the jeep, so I mumbled something, not daring to turn my head to give a proper answer. Steering I could do, but I didn't know how to shift gears. So, I proceeded in first gear, with the officer in the back seat repeatedly pointing to the shift stick, wondering what was going on and probably wondering why I didn't know how to drive properly.

As we proceeded, we came to a crossroads. Another jeep full of soldiers approached on my right, but I had no clue they had the right of way. I plowed through the intersection right into them. It was a good thing I was in first gear. I hadn't caused much damage. A couple of military police rolled up in their own jeep and all of them began yelling at me, calling me the idiot of the century.

The MPs asked for my driver's license. I told him I didn't have one, so they hauled me to their station and called my commander.

Eventually, it came out that I had been commanded to drive by the officer, so they let me off with a light reprimand. At the time, I didn't think it was very amusing.

After basic infantry training was finished after about two months, I was sent back to Camp Ritchie in Maryland. I was taught security, censorship, sabotage operations, explosives and an overview of how the German hierarchy worked, including the rankings in their military.

I despised training in fire prevention. They set fire to a number of boxes in the field and showed us how to spray chemicals on them to extinguish the fire. It really annoyed me. One day they announced the arrival of a couple of FBI men who were going to teach us the art of self-defense. They dressed as German soldiers and demonstrated moves in jujitsu we had to practice. I was still thinking about flying, so I asked for a transfer. They quite literally laughed at me because there was no such thing as transferring from infantry to the Air Force.

Eventually, I finally got orders. Scanning through the strange language and incomprehensible abbreviations, the words "flight school" caught my attention. They were directing me to basic flight training at Punta Gorda Army Airfield in Florida. I was in heaven.

CHAPTER 21

Flying

WHEN I SHOWED the orders to my Lieutenant, he started calling whoever wrote them "total idiots." I was only a private in the infantry and had been trained in counterintelligence, but I think it's possible that my faithful friend, Captain Claude, remembered how, back in France, I had talked nonstop about my desire to pilot airplanes. Also, apparently Claude had a lot of power at Army Intelligence and possibly even at the War Department. So, my orders were confirmed and I was as happy as a clam.

The whole experience at Punta Gorda Army Airfield in Florida was one of the happiest times of my life. Rain or shine, every day was a feast of new discoveries. My tent may have leaked at times and the food in the mess hall may have been "el stinko," but I was going to fly and nothing else mattered. There was a great sense of camaraderie among us cadets; even though some complained about the many discomforts, we all were completely dedicated to our tasks and elated to perform them.

Once theory classes were over, we actually got to sit at the controls of a Boeing-Stearman biplane trainer. I was thrilled but then became nervous to the point I was shaking all over. Suddenly, an accident I had witnessed, where a student pilot erred, crashed and was killed came flooding back to me. Could I avoid a similar fate? Tom, my flight instructor told me to take it easy and stop shaking, which I was unable to do. The biplane looked huge and heavy. Despite my newly acquired knowledge of the theory of flight, I wasn't convinced that I could get this "crate" to go up into the sky.

Tom started the engine, and it came alive with a roar. The noise was deafening, though somewhat muffled by my leather flying cap. The noise increased my fears. It brought back the memory of the uneasy feeling I had during my first flight from France. All this changed the moment we were airborne and Tom told me to take the stick. With my feet firmly planted on the rudder pedals and stick in hands, I finally satisfied a lifelong wish – control of an airplane. A feeling of total exhilaration came over me. I was no longer a flying cadet. I had become a bird!

Instantly, the airplane and I became one. I understood her and she understood me. I had no further need for my instructor; I flew the plane by instinct. It still scared me to look down at the earth, but the pressure of the pilot's seat against my buttocks gave me a feeling of safety. During my flight training, I spent some 60 hours in the open cockpit of the Stearman. In the beginning, I was scared to death, but later I grew to enjoy every minute of it. Instruction in instrument flying and cross-country navigation in the more powerful BT-13 Vultee followed. I was glad for the radio compass on the dashboard because I had no innate sense of direction.

In time, I lost my fear of threatening cloud formations and I concentrated on the spaces of sky between them, revealing the stark, yet colorful earth below. When I first dared to push the stick forward to dive into these crevices in the air, I did so hesitantly and at a very shallow angle. Later, as I gained skill and confidence, I dived much deeper and pulled out much steeper. Pulling my machine up with the resulting G-forces gave me so much joy it overcame all fear during flight.

I also completed training for twin-engine flight in a Cessna AT-17. This had been a tough experience resulting in several near-crashes. I eventually earned my wings and was sent by train, bus, and army truck to an airport for multiple-engine and flight training as well as photo interpretation at Pecos Army Airfield in Texas. There, I was introduced to the famous fighter plane, the Lockheed Lightning P-38 F5B. However, this aircraft was the stripped-down version, with four cameras equipped with Bausch & Lomb lenses for photoreconnaissance replacing the armament. In the cockpit on the bottom was an instrument called an intervalometer which controlled the distortion due to the speed of the aircraft. I had a hard time grasping how to work it properly; it was a little beyond me.

My flying days were short-lived. In the inscrutable reasoning of the military, they ignored all my flight training and aerial photography work. Instead of building on that, they ordered me back to Camp Ritchie.

CHAPTER 22

Back to Europe

Back in Maryland, counterintelligence training continued. We learned lock picking, how to take fingerprints, and procedures to prevent or control the communications of a municipality. The first step was to cut telephone wires and then to seal off post offices by stationing guards. After a while, I graduated and was sent off to a theatre in Chicago, Illinois, for the ceremony. Suddenly, a melody began and everybody stood at attention and saluted. I was confused and figured something important was happening, so I followed suit. I later laughed at myself because I was hearing the American national anthem for the first time in my life. Now, I was officially a member of the United States Counterintelligence Corps with my War Department credentials.

From there, we were transferred to Camp Wolters in Mineral Wells, Texas, where I was assigned to the 970th CIC (Counterintelligence Corps) Detachment, which in turn was attached to the 90th Infantry Division, named The Texas – Oklahoma Division or "TO," as the shoulder patches on our uniforms revealed. GIs from all over the country were in this division, and somehow we became known as the Tough Hombres instead of the TO division. The chow was terrible and our spirits were low. We struggled through weeks of arduous training and field maneuvers with a full pack on our backs, toiling through the burning hot desert. I suffered from heat prostration and complained about everything, like the other GI's. In a way, however, I didn't really mean it. Compared to constantly hiding out in Holland and France with the Germans on my tail, this was a piece of cake.

I only complained because I wanted to fit in and didn't want to be considered a foreigner. I never let anyone know I was Dutch, so when asked, "Where are you from?" my standard line was I was from California. When pressed further, I would say, "Glendale." I was lucky to get away with this, as I never met anyone outside of my team that was from there. I had always fantasized about being American, and now I was actually passing as one.

During our intense training, I got to know Ray Lustig who was in his late twenties and had a pockmarked face. His hometown was Detroit, and when I finally did let him know I was born in Rotterdam, he began singing some folk song about "The Rotterdam Dutch" that I'd never heard of before. I didn't know much about his background then, but over time learned about his life back home. Ray never talked too much anyway, but he became one of my closer friends on the team.

We trained and sweated a lot. On top of our gruesome training from sunrise to sunset, we were not allowed to leave the camp, which meant no excursions off base. Our only form of entertainment was the movies shown on weekends. For some unknown reason, I was chosen to operate the movie projector, which I liked very much.

Our Captain was Walter D. Osborne, Commanding Officer. He was from Orange County, California, and had an amazing personality. He took a great liking to me, and I idolized him. Tall and fair-haired with a blonde moustache, he could recite Shakespeare with ease while standing on a stool. In civilian life, he'd been a correspondent for *Time* magazine; I believe he covered the civil war in Spain. He started teaching me Spanish, which he was fluent in. He granted me the nickname "Dr. Nookie" then promoted me to "Professor Nookie." He reserved "Mr. Eigenheimer" for when he thought I was being an argumentative wise guy.

We soon realized that all our training was to prepare us for ground warfare in Europe. Although it felt scary, it stiffened my purpose. I had many a score left to settle with the Germans who still were persecuting my people. They didn't ship us east from Texas to our port of debarkation by fancy transportation. We suffered through endless train rides intermingled with uncomfortable trips in army trucks. On the way, we slept in tents or barracks, dragging our heavy, over-brimming duffle bags, bedrolls and helmets. After seven days on the road, we finally reached the port of New York, where we were to embark for Europe.

As far as the eye could see, the port was jammed with ships of all sorts and sizes. Each division had its own staging area for its men to board their ship. Nonetheless, the area was a scene of confusion. Thousands of GIs were milling around, joking and complaining. Ultimately, my unit ended up in the right place and moved onto the gangplank of our assigned ship. It was something like the USS *Primrose,* or some other flower-sounding name. You'd think I would have remembered the name, given the importance and serious nature of the trip; however, I can't recall it to this day. I do know it was considered a Liberty ship which held between 1,000 and 2,000 of us GIs.

As the ship left its mooring, I looked for the Statue of Liberty, but I never caught sight of her. Come to think of it, it's surprising – I have made countless trips to New York on business and pleasure, and I never did see that lady. As a grateful visitor, I might have tried harder to see her in person. On the passage to England, I was getting pangs of both anxiety and anticipation. The crossing was amazingly uneventful. We soldiers were stacked on berths in the inner hold of the ship, four tiers high. So, the sleeping accommodations were terrible and so was the food.

"Lousy mush," a soldier remarked, looking at what was dumped on his tray at chow time. A sergeant, overhearing this, shot back sarcastically, "Brother, you never had it so good!" That expression came to be used a lot, including when it came to our frustration with the toilet facilities. They were unable to handle the traffic of thousands of GIs lining up to wash or shower, and the resulting body odor made our lives miserable. During the day, we whiled away the time with endless games of craps. I didn't take part; I just watched. Even today, I don't understand how that game worked. GIs threw money around like there was no tomorrow, which, in fact, was a thought occupying our minds.

We knew we were on our way to war and we couldn't help wondering – would we make it? Despite the feeling of uncertainty, I didn't focus on that thought. Other GIs lay on their bunks, staring into nothingness, chain-smoking one cigarette after another. Others camouflaged their concern in the opposite extreme – acting boisterously and rowdy with an air of great indifference, but they were not very convincing. As a reminder of what they had left behind, almost every man pinned photos of loved ones to the wall or to the bottom of the mattress of the buddy who bunked on top of them.

When I pondered what might lay ahead, I focused on the pleasure of sticking it to the Nazis. I imagined slowly maiming one of the bastards up close. I had learned to fire at the enemy through long-range weapons, but I wanted to see them suffer right in front of me. I imagined taking a .45-caliber pistol and shooting one of them in the ear, then the hand. Next, I'd put a few bullets into his knees and feet. I'd tie up one of his buddies, and make him watch as the first one lay bleeding on the ground. Then I would torture the second guy the same way. This imaginary scenario gave me great satisfaction and fueled my desire for revenge. I was actually looking forward to getting into action against our enemy. The memory of the oppression I had suffered was still fresh in my mind.

We were zigzagging our way across the Atlantic to avoid enemy submarines, so at least 10 days passed before the coast of England finally appeared on the horizon. It was April 5, 1944, and we ended up in the city of Birmingham. Must be a different place; Birmingham is in the Midlands, the center of Britain.

The state of confusion prior to our boarding in New York repeated itself during debarkation. There was lots of shoving and maneuvering of thousands of GIs. At one point, I even ended up going to a training school in Blackpool only to be told I was in the wrong place. Endless truck and train rides followed until our division came to a stop near Birmingham. We parked out of town for two days and nights with trucks, jeeps and trailers lined bumper to bumper on both sides of the country roads.

People in the nearby village were friendly and treated us to afternoon tea, plying us with cakes and other goodies. One family, the Slades, even invited me into their home for dinner and gave me a place to sleep in an attic room. Instead of bunking on a cot in a tent or sleeping on the seat of a jeep, I could sleep in a soft bed with clean, white sheets. In the morning, the breakfast Mrs. Slade served me was unforgettable: toast grilled in oil drippings. It tasted wonderful.

On the third day in the area, our division moved on to a proper camp. It had tents and barracks for soldiers and metal igloos for the officers. Our CIC detachment was lucky; instead of assigning us to tents, we were given quarters on the second floor of a solid building. We were assigned to counterintelligence duties in line with our mandate. We were issued U.S. officers' emblems to pin on our shirt collars and ordered to remove the rank insignia from our sleeves and replace them with a CIC armband. Most of us had been issued brown parachute boots, and with our get-up, so many people took us for officers instead of enlisted men. GIs usually gave us the salute, which we returned, whereas officers gave us a quizzical look, not knowing what to make of us.

Each man in our unit received a dark blue, leather-bound identification booklet. Printed in English, French, German and Russian, it described our function and authority using wording that gave us practically carte blanche to do what we needed. Beneath our photograph and signature, it read to the effect of: "This is to certify that the person whose picture appears in this document is a Special Agent of the Counterintelligence Corps and is authorized to perform such duties as may be entrusted to him."

Along with the booklet, we received a gold-plated badge issued by the War Department, a pocket fingerprint set, a leather pouch with a set of small tools to pick locks, a colt .38 mm, a short-nosed revolver in a shoulder holster, and a Thompson submachine gun. Our unit had its own portable crime investigation lab in a trailer that we could set up anywhere in short order. We had a high-level security clearance. However, they limited my personal security clearance since I was only 20 at the time, the youngest member of the team. I was allowed to see documents classified as confidential and secret – but not Top Secret or For Your Eyes Only.

The CIC, along with the rest of the American forces, were in full training during the months of April and May 1944. We were scheduled to conduct operations on the European mainland behind the primary invasion force, considered the "rear echelon." By the end of May, we expected the invasion to happen soon because general orders were issued, canceling all leave and allowing no one off base.

The boys in our motor pool received orders to completely wax the engines of our vehicles and attach upright conduits to the tailpipes. This made our jeeps look ridiculous, but we realized the reason: our jeeps and the other vehicles of the landing force would be offloaded in shallow water once we crossed the Channel. I also realized that the modifications meant that it might only be a few days before the invasion would actually start.

All communication was prohibited, for both civilians and military personnel. This led to our first wide-ranging CIC job: to prevent and counteract any enemy espionage and sabotage in the country. This meant we had to close civilian post offices and silence telephone exchanges. After we sealed off post offices, military police stationed themselves there to prevent any further use. Even our soldiers themselves were restricted. We could receive incoming mail, but outgoing mail was held back.

We faced our most serious challenge in closing down civilian radio shortwave operators in Britain. Local constabularies and police were requested to submit lists of owners so we could interview them and, if necessary, impound their apparatus. When we confronted a local constable, we encountered stiff resistance. The man in charge did not believe we had the right to interrogate British citizens or impound British property, stating that the American Army was not an occupying force on British soil. He tried to remind us we were merely guests that had no right to enter British homes or limit the activities of British citizens. We attempted to remind him that they were residing in a military zone, and that we were in the war effort together – but we failed. They refused to cooperate, so we informed the British military at top echelons, and the British army took over this potential leak in our security.

The atmosphere became thicker and heavier by the hour. The invasion was imminent. People had to cover their ears to dampen the drone of motors from the equipment moving on the ground and in the air. Thousands of vehicles were on the move, clogging the narrow English coastal roads. Airplanes and white cylindrical balloons darkened the sky. The familiar butterflies crept back into my stomach. We could sense something colossal was about to happen.

We had no specific advance notice of when or where our forces were going to land in continental Europe. We CIC agents were instructed to follow behind the advancing troops and enforce our rules in the occupied or liberated war zones. Our instructions were specific:

1. Disable all telephone traffic by cutting wires and sealing off exchanges.
2. Seal off all postal offices and facilities and block mail and telegraph traffic.
3. Arrest and imprison all persons suspected of collaboration with the enemy.
4. Interrogate prisoners of war and identify those suspected of war crimes.
5. Gather intelligence from enemy positions and submit relevant data to Army Intelligence.

Early on the morning of June 6, 1944, we learned that elements of our 90th Infantry Division had already landed in Normandy, France on, a beach called "Utah." Our unit was told to load our vehicles on a landing craft and be ready to move across the Channel on June 8, 1944. At the time, I didn't understand much about the military and had no idea which U.S. Army we served under. However, after the initial landings in Normandy, the division came under the command of General George Patton who commanded the U.S. Third Army.

CHAPTER 23

Facing the Enemy

IT WAS CLEAR that this was it. When I stood in line for breakfast, I noticed nobody seemed to have an appetite. Everyone looked somber and scared, including me. The familiar butterflies were back in my stomach. We had not been informed of the heavy fighting and casualties the first troops that landed in the days before. We had all seen movies about war and felt it – death and destruction, fear and danger, blood and wounds – they were an impending reality.

During my basic training at Fort Benning, instructors sometimes used live ammunition to bring the reality of war close to us. Bullets were fired so close to my head I could feel the air vibrate in my ears and cheeks. I got the message: "Don't lift your head an inch, or you're dead." It was eerie and frightful, and done on purpose.

Now, here at our base in England, I tried to internalize the destruction the weaponry I had learned to use could inflict. I lifted my pillow and stared intensely at the colt revolver I kept there. The weapon itself did not frighten me, but when I imagined some similar weapon pointed at me, my stomach revolted. I wondered what it would feel like to be living one second and dead a split second later because someone pulled a trigger. My thoughts turned to those who committed suicide by revolver – cases of bodies found dead with a gun in their hand. Did these people kill themselves because they hated to live, or were they just curious to find out what it was like to pass over the great divide between life and death? My mind raced in a million directions.

After breakfast on that fateful day, we boarded the landing craft – an LCT (Landing Craft Tank) to which Ray Lustig and I had been assigned – and received our final orders. An officer explained that our ship would approach the Normandy beach as close as possible. The bow doors would open and the landing ramp would lower. The tanks and half-tracks, which were loaded last, would be the first ones out and would provide cover for the smaller vehicles that followed. Our preparations would allow the engines to keep functioning in shallow water; our jeeps' engines were sealed with wax and the exhaust pipes were extended up past water levels so the engines would not drown.

When the giant panels of the ship started to close, I felt like we were being locked in, with no possibility of escape. I felt the vibration of the powerful engines starting up. We were moving and there was no way out. I said to myself, "If it has to be, let it be. I am committed." I was 20 years old and had come a long way from being a shy teen, hunted for the crime of being a Jew in my occupied city of Rotterdam. I was returning to Europe, with the power of an Allied army behind me. I felt invincible and scared shitless at the same time.

I don't remember much about the crossing – we couldn't see anything. When we got close to the beach, the landings began. Ray Lustig was waiting for me, sitting at the wheel of our jeep, where he had painted "Cindy" on the side, proudly named after his wife. I jumped in the front seat with two others in the back.

Soon we heard our ship's keel scrape bottom and with a loud roar, the onboard tank engines started and began to blow exhaust smoke into the rear of the ship where our jeeps were waiting. The air became blue and stifling; we could barely breathe. The noise was overwhelming, echoing against the steel hull of the landing craft. Tank after tank rolled down the ramp like a giant monster. The halftracks and trucks followed.

Then it was our turn. Seawater surged into our jeep as we rolled down the ramp. I remember the terror inside of me. We didn't speak at all; we held our breath. We looked at one another, unable to say anything, water soaking us up to our knees. Outside, we saw a clear sky and, to our surprise, we heard no shooting. Even so, I ducked my head as deep as I could because I was dead scared and expected to be killed instantly.

As it turned out, our LCT had landed on the wrong section of the beachhead. The landing craft had drifted too far to the right side of the section called "Red Fox," where we were supposed to land. As a result, we couldn't find our command post. Someone pointed us to the left, putting us back in the right direction. In the confusion that ensued, I saw no sign of enemy resistance. No enemy fire, no German soldiers.

Since we were some 2,000 yards off from our planned landing site, the actual fighting was 12 miles ahead of us. This was a stroke of luck because our segment of Utah Beach was not as heavily defended as the location where we were supposed to land. Also, in direct line ahead, our paratroopers had fought to liberate Sainte-Mère-Église just a few days before.

I was still keeping my head down. When I finally dared to look up, I saw the immense devastation caused by the previous landings. Landing ships and vehicles ripped apart or still burning and smoking lay in grotesque heaps of steel on the beach and in the surf. What frightened me most were the body bags I saw stacked up when we finally reached our destination.

Of course, observing body bags was nothing as gruesome as when I saw actual dead bodies up close. It was grisly. The first time I saw four dead German soldiers frozen in time with their heads split open in front of a burned-up tank, it gave me an odd pleasure as these were my enemies. But the first time I saw a dead GI, my heart crunched in pain and tears came to my eyes.

La Haye-du-Puits was the first village sign I remember. Soon, I was meeting the French locals. They were overjoyed to be free of the German occupation and its excesses, and they didn't know how to do enough to make us feel welcomed. They hugged and kissed us and handed us bottles of wine. I was one of the few in my division who spoke French, and I took the lead in reciprocating our welcome. I was proud to be the recipient of such gratitude, and my heart swelled to be part of this liberating army.

It is well known that in this vast undertaking, thousands of fighting men lost their lives. However, I can say that I was loving my life in the army. The army had become my father and mother – my family.

It gave me a sense of home, providing food, shelter, and security and that meant the world to a young man my age, who was alone in the world and whose youth had been stolen by the Nazis.

As soon as the 90th Division of Patton's Third Army had taken the first city in France, my CIC group went to city hall to get the mayor to report on the local situation. We sealed post offices and telephone exchanges as instructed, and we moved all persons of a suspicious nature out of the area so Nazi collaborators could be sorted out later.

We were operating in the rear, but nonetheless, a few days after D-Day, a mortar landed near me. I was sitting on my helmet talking to three other GIs when the force of the explosion sent me into the air. I landed on my back and I got up, groggy and disoriented. I looked around for my three buddies. Nothing. They had disappeared into thin air. Not a shred was left of them. It was shocking, and it was obvious that even the rear echelon wasn't safe from the horrid destruction of war.

Towards the end of August 1944, we arrived in Le Mans. I was standing on a hill overlooking a scene of major destruction. The German army had been severely defeated. Over 10,000 dead soldiers, dead horses, and thousands of vehicles – trucks and tanks – and equipment – cannons and artillery – had been blasted into junk. Here over 40,000 German soldiers had surrendered and been taken prisoner. Only the nauseating stench of death and devastation remained. We had arrived in time to witness the aftermath of the Battle of the Falaise Gap.

After our victory at Falaise, Patton's troops advanced so far ahead of schedule that we in the CIC quickly fell behind in our work. We had to deal with countless new French cities and villages, too many to handle for our 20 CIC agents plus 10 soldiers in our motor pool. Therefore, we decided to split our group up by sending just a two-man team to each liberated locality.

Ray Lustig and I formed one such team and covered a broad territory to close an endless number of post offices and telephone exchanges. On one occasion, as we were walking, a mortar exploded near us. After the booming sound and shock subsided, we realized we were not hurt, but a big piece of cardboard eerily floated in the air and landed almost on top of me.

We needed MPs to make sure the post offices stayed sealed, but soon there were no more MPs available. So, we deputized French resistance agents to take over. We didn't have enough time for lengthy investigations. We arrested anyone on the slightest suspicion of being a spy, Nazi collaborator or war criminal. Without many preliminaries, we put them behind bars. We ordered them held there until an interrogation team following behind us could dig into their past and determine their proper disposition.

My work assignments burgeoned. I now had a chance to deal with big-shot Nazis, not low-level conscripts. I also saw how war had created thousands of displaced persons. In one town, we were quartered in a huge building that once had accommodated German soldiers. Every other building in town was rubble. We were happy to find this one building that remained standing even though it had no electricity. It had several floors and was divided into two wings with the main entrance in the center.

The right wing of the building was occupied by hundreds of refugees of all ages and nationalities. We were quartered in the left wing. Hundreds of GIs lay stretched out on blankets and bedrolls on the floor. Using flashlights to help us step over these early arrivals, we found ourselves some space to bed down. Mike, one of the soldiers who was a friend of mine and had gotten to the place before us went to the other wing, where the refugees were. He encountered a group of Polish girls. He crossed back to our side, all excited about these attractive girls, and offered to bring me back there.

Naturally, that sparked my interest and in no time, I was hanging out with a group of girls lounging on the floor. Mike was already busily handing out cigarettes and candy. The girls spoke only Polish, but we didn't let that bother us. I walked up to a cute girl and started talking with short words and hand signals. Soon I was crouching on the floor next to her. I remember two words she taught me: "*pocałunek*," kiss, and "*papieros*," cigarettes.

Other soldiers came over to be with the girls. It was cold in the building and they brought blankets which soon covered the entire group. Interests other than cigarettes and candy soon took over. In the quiet, the only sounds were occasional moans and sighs. Despite the blankets, it got too cold for me. I tried to tell my girl the best I could that I was going to fetch my warm bedroll and extra blankets. When I returned to our wing, Captain Osborn, our commander, spotted me and asked where I was going. I winked and told him I was going back to the cute girls in the other wing.

"Nothing doing," he said and ordered me to stay put. After I curled up in my warm bedroll, German artillery began firing. I heard it in my sleep, but being used to that kind of noise, I slept right through it. The next morning, I was shocked to find the entire right wing had been blown up while I was asleep. It had taken a direct hit – I was just lucky to have been ordered not to return. I never found out if Mike or my girl had made it out alive. That was the nature of war.

We were driving along in a small town in France with our CIC convoy – more than ten jeeps, a truck (with personnel and equipment) and a command car – and we all stopped for lunch. As I was eating my K-ration, I caught sight of a complete flight of P-38s parked in a distant airfield. I couldn't contain my excitement and drove up to get a better look. When I went inside the command post to talk shop with the pilots there, I told them that I had been trained in a P-38 during my days attached to the Army Air Corps and I hoped to get to pilot a P-38 again.

They suggested I arrange a few days of leave and fly to England for some R&R with them. I went back to my commanding officer, Captain Osborn, and he arranged for me to get a pass. When I was all set to go and returned to the airbase, the pilots explained that there was no chance for me to fly a P-38. In fact, I wouldn't get to do any piloting whatsoever. They explained that since we weren't heading out on a mission, they couldn't authorize flying four planes across the Channel and we would be heading out on a C-47 transport plane instead.

Crash-landing

About five or ten minutes after takeoff, an explosion shook the aircraft. I was sitting behind the rear door near the tail section and felt a burning on the right side of my face. Stunned from the blast, I looked up and saw a gaping hole near the tail of the aircraft, and the rudder was hanging out of kilter on the fuselage. Somehow, the pilot was able to crash-land the crippled plane, although I have no idea how he did it. Whatever hit us in midair also remained a mystery, and it was a miracle we survived the crash. All of us on board walked away, with minor burns, cuts and scratches, save the pilot, who also broke his foot.

A military ambulance took us to a field hospital, a huge installation of tents covering a wide area. It was equipped with everything a modern hospital needed and was staffed by a devoted group of surgeons and nurses. I was treated for burns on my face, left arm and thighs. My worst injury was the burn on the right side of my face, which had singed my eyebrow and eyelashes off. They kept me as an ambulatory patient for four days, and upon my discharge from the field hospital, in a short ceremony, they awarded me with a Purple Heart, a decoration for injury in battle.

In September, we reached Fontainebleau, which was not far from Pamfou, and I was anxious to go there to see my girlfriend Esther, the mayor Jean and others. I had not been able to contact anyone there since I suddenly left Pamfou with Claude. We were forbidden to travel alone, so Ray had to ride with me – only he didn't want to go. We still had a lot of territory to cover, and he wanted to get on with the work. In the end, he grumblingly agreed to come along. Halfway there, we ran into small arms fire and we had to take cover. I was disappointed, but the risk of injury was greater than the benefit of seeing my old friends, so we had to return to our command post on safer ground.

The 90th Infantry troops liberated one city after another, and we followed shortly behind once the fighting was over. When we reached Reims in August, the Champagne City, bubbly was flowing like tap water at parties all over the newly liberated city. I didn't drink any because I didn't like the stuff and I wasn't a drinker. Restaurants and bars opened their doors and doled out food and drinks to all. I don't think there was a single enlisted man or officer in town who stayed sober besides me. I witnessed four soldiers turn a corner so fast, their jeep flipped on its side. I guess alcohol acted as a painkiller because they didn't seem seriously hurt; they promptly got up, righted the jeep and went on their merry way.

At Reims, we felt that we were advancing so fast with practically no resistance. We were euphoric in believing the war was almost over. This feeling came to an abrupt halt when we reached the city of Metz, where the entire third Army ran out of gas. It seemed the war was almost over and the whole army went mad, and so did the local population. For about a week, we were in this holding pattern and got wind of German resistance strengthening.

You couldn't see the sky anymore; there was nothing but hundreds of C-47 transport planes parachuting in thousands of gasoline drums so we could continue our drive into Germany. We were on the move again, and soon Ray and I were crossing the Moselle River under fire in September 1944.

By December, we were near the Belgian border and, in the middle of the night – Christmas eve – our field phone awakened us. When I answered, we were ordered to evacuate immediately and follow the main convoy, which was already on the move. We struggled out of our sleeping bags (even with their cleverly engineered quick release zippers), tried to pack as fast as we could, and loaded our gear into our trucks and trailers. We sensed something ominous was happening even though we didn't know what.

The winter of 1944, was one of the most severe on record. We couldn't escape the bitter cold riding in our open jeeps, blinded by the freezing wind as we passed through small towns and villages. We drove without lights because of strict blackout orders. The roads were slippery, so many jeeps and trucks in the convoy got into collisions. Our jeep stayed intact, even though we also bumped into the rear of the jeep in front of us one time.

I sat in the back seat of our jeep, getting the worst of the paralyzing wind. Even though I wore long johns and packed blankets all around me, I still froze. Ray was driving, and with the windshield as protection, he got less of a beating, but soon all four of us in our jeep couldn't feel our toes anymore. I huddled against a buddy silently; it was too cold to open our mouths to speak. We drove through the night and into most of the morning. We only stopped for gas and piss calls. Later GIs were saying, "It was so cold, we pissed ice cubes."

Sometime in the late morning, our convoy was halted and our CIC group got a signal to proceed on our own. We didn't get very far, miserable as we were from utter cold and exhaustion. Without even looking for a bite to eat, we stopped at a farm with a large, covered haystack. I jumped into the hay, wrapped all my blankets around me, and immediately fell into a deep sleep.

CHAPTER 24

Entering Nazi Germany

THROUGH A SERIES of unexpected events, German forces failed to blow up the Ludendorff Bridge spanning the Rhine River at Remagen. This provided a direct path into the heart of Germany. We entered German territory in the first months of 1945. That, of course, was a big step for me – even the boots on my feet hated that country. The Nazi regime had created such an intense system of hatred that indoctrinated men, women and children. Ordinary citizens lived in fear and pressure from their own government, bound by strict rules and harsh punishments. All the German houses now displayed white flags and, oddly enough, they appeared as cowards; they were afraid of us.

All doors were shut. No people were visible. Those we did see were either very young or very old; almost everyone in between were obviously off to war, fighting our troops on the remaining fronts. The people must have been afraid of us, having been told we were going to harm them – but eventually they found out we were decent people. Children especially were friendly and we gave them chocolates and candies – much appreciated treats during a time of food shortages and rations. Our CIC work became more difficult. Who would assist us in finding Nazis and war criminals? In France, it wasn't hard to find resistance fighters or people who had avoided enemy collaboration to helped us find the goons we needed to bring to justice. On German soil, who could we trust?

I had to force myself to speak German, a language I knew fairly well but thoroughly hated. However, I had the support of my buddies, and we started to randomly knock on doors to find people willing to talk to us. Eventually, headquarters passed us a list identifying known war criminals and the hunt was on to find them. The work was hard. Nobody we challenged ever admitted to being a Nazi or even having known one. Resistance to our inquiries was strong – people constantly denied any wrongdoing. Ironically, we got the most help from the local German police. We were in the same profession, and professional courtesy required them to be more or less willing to work with us.

Our other source of help was human nature; our training had taught us to use hatred, greed and jealousy to our advantage. We could get a person to talk about someone they were jealous of or they carried a grudge against after a few minutes of gentle interrogation. Greed usually existed between the haves and the have-nots, and we exploited that as well. Gradually the results of our work improved as we learned more about the German mentality and how they responded to authority.

Once ordinary German civilians realized they were now free of the pressures the Nazis had imposed, they became more open towards us. Their animosity decreased when they found out their own government had lied to them about almost everything and that we Americans were not the rapists and savages that they had been led to believe. Through interrogating everyday folks, I learned a lot about how the Nazis had mistreated their own people – cajoled, forced and even executed them to force them into adopting the party line. In many cases, even people who had no love for the Nazis were forced to act against their will. The regime forced people to spy on their neighbors and friends, and report on their activities.

The Nazi sympathizers we uncovered usually were older Germans who were happy with Hitler. They felt poor and underprivileged, motivated by jealousy and hatred for the Jews whom they believed deprived them of their "rightful Teutonic heritage." The Nazi propaganda machine fanned anti-Semitism and spread it all over Germany. All day long, every medium of communication proclaimed Jews were rats and vermin. In short, the Nazis knew how to take plain folks and convert them into solid believers or close collaborators.

One bright, insightful woman I spoke with described it well: the sentiment of the Nazi era was that if you didn't like Hitler, *you* were the enemy. He was the one you had to thank for rescuing the Fatherland from poverty by creating jobs for the unemployed. He was the one who saved the nation from Communism. He was the one who devised the Volkswagen, and who built a string of Autobahns to tie the nation together. *Heil Hitler!*

The most insidious aspect of Nazi propaganda was its indoctrination of the youth. In England, I had gotten to know the influence of the Boy Scout movement created by Lord Baden-Powell ("BP" as he was popularly known). This movement gave young boys a uniform, friendship and discipline while teaching respect. It wasn't militaristic; it taught good manners and created an oath to do at least one good deed per day.

Hitler and his gang cleverly co-opted the Boy Scouts, renaming the movement as the *Hitler-Jugend* (Hitler-Youth Group) and turning it into a semi-military organization. It trained boys to become soldiers and indoctrinated them in Nazi ideology. Instead of doing a good deed once a day, they were told to defend the Fatherland and have a knife ready for every Jew.

Leaders of the *Hitler-Jugend* were excellent raw material to later become SS officers. As I interrogated and analyzed the mindset of these young men, I found most of them too fanatical to listen to reason. Sadly, they had no concept of normal human values or civilized behavior. They had been brainwashed to believe white was black no matter what their own eyes told them. Many were so indoctrinated that they had no scruples remaining and appeared to have no issues operating the gas chambers in concentration camps. They became firmly convinced that Jews were parasites of society and rapists of German maidens. The German people were so completely misled – and the fallout was death and destruction.

By April 1945, we were stationed in the city of Gotha, where we found an abandoned Gestapo residence to stay in temporarily. The officers had fled in great haste, leaving their personal articles behind. Because they had confiscated the best homes, the rooms were richly furnished and laden with the finest perfumes, foods and liquor. I opened many wardrobes stuffed full with the finest silk dresses, clearly from famous Parisian clothiers. All this decadence stood in direct contrast to the general population, who had very little and struggled to put food on the table. I also discovered a gallery of pornography, which revealed male homosexual relationships that would have been kept hidden.

CHAPTER 25

Nuremberg, 1945

FROM BAMBERG, WE headed into Nuremberg sometime in late March or early April 1945. We arrived in our jeeps in the early afternoon to find the streets deserted, the inner city totally destroyed and many windows displaying white flags, fashioned from bed sheets or other white material. This was the German civilians' message of surrender.

I remember that day as mild, allowing us to lower the canvas cover of our jeeps to get a better view of our surroundings. Our small convoy consisted of 10 jeeps, three of them pulling trailers, and two small trucks. We parked on the outskirts of the city. and I took pictures with a camera I had "liberated" from a dead German soldier. Soon we found ourselves in front of 27 Wieland Strasse, the former Gestapo headquarters.

The building was divided into a first floor for offices, and the second floor for living quarters. The basement contained a fully equipped kitchen capable of entertaining many guests. There were also shower stalls and three windowless, sparsely furnished rooms with heavy doors – holding rooms for prisoners. The first floor at the rear looked out over a white slatted balcony with stairs leading down to an inner garden. Heavy shrubbery surrounded the space, making it impossible for outsiders to look inside.

A large swimming pool with no water in it and full of dead leaves sat in the middle of the garden. Once we got all our personal belongings out of the jeeps and trailers, we soon found out that the place did not have enough room to house all of us. For the first couple of days, we all bunked together, two or three to a room. There was a grand piano on the second floor and one of our agents, Jay Pfotenhouser, turned out to be a good player and would serenade us.

We finally found a beautiful building in Fürth for living quarters. I was lucky and got the top floor, which had a beautiful green and white glazed stone fireplace from floor to ceiling. It had a bed, a place for my radio and a gramophone with a collection of classical symphony records, mostly Bach.

Our new commanding officer who'd taken over from Osborne, was Special Agent Captain Ernest Yarnevich, a jovial man in his forties, over six feet tall with receding hair. He was unpretentious and friendly. In civilian life, he was a lawyer from Kansas City and, thanks to his Polish parents, he spoke Polish fluently. "Yarny," as we called him, was soon busy setting up offices with equipment and getting field telephones installed by the fellows from Signal Corps. He must have known Nuremberg was going to be our permanent place of business.

One of my buddies was Leo Trykowski, whom we called "Tryk." He was not a CIC agent, but a soldier assigned to our motor pool, helping with general duties, like picking up supplies and groceries. His hometown was Pittsburgh. He was tall, skinny and around the same age as I. Being the two youngest on the team, he would often invite me along to ride on some errands. We played baseball and football, and did a fair amount of partying and chasing girls – even smuggling some into our CIC offices. We found a small dog that we took care of and called Jale, a combination of our names, Jack and Leo.

On April 12, 1945, a few of us were ordered to form a security guard for General Dwight D. Eisenhower and his staff during a visit to a place called Ohrdruf. We learned it was a forced labor camp – a "concentration camp," – that our troops had liberated the week prior. Omar Bradley, General George S. Patton, General Clark, other officials and the international press were going to be there as well. I was assigned as one of the security guards for the top brass.

When we arrived, Eisenhower's own security detail kept us away from him. We were trying to figure out what we should be doing when the reality of the place hit me. This cauldron of suffering, pain and death permeated the haunting atmosphere and overwhelmed all of us. I felt a the stench of death choke me, and a dread gnawing my insides. I looked around for answers, not believing my eyes. Wherever I looked I saw things my mind was unable to accept. *This is impossible*, I thought. *This is not real.* How could humans be capable of this?

At this disturbing place, the Nazis accessed hell and transferred it to Earth intact. They created the devils needed to operate their inferno with evil and damnation. I totally lost my belief in a so-called merciful God there, though I always had great doubts about religion itself. Words have not been invented to describe the horror. It was so overwhelming with no space to think clearly; disbelief in what my eyes were trying to understand. It's understandable that Eisenhower ordered members of the press to record and document what they witnessed there. He wanted to ensure that no one could dispute the utter cruelty of the human condition.

The realization of how lucky I was hit hard; there were many times I narrowly escaped ending up at a camp like this. The total depravity and the degeneration of the human being in this place was so brutal, cruel and severe that Eisenhower's body protested, and he vomited. I had to look away or I would have been sick, too. I wondered about the fate of my family back in Holland, but I had no ability to get news from them or let them know that I had survived and was okay.

When we got back to Nuremberg, word got out about someone on our team who had discovered a bottle of Slivovitz. It was some type of Polish or Slovakian plum brandy with an extremely high alcohol content. Special Agent John Slater, second in command with a pale complexion, and dirty blonde hair, partook of the stuff. I had never seen him drink anything more potent than a beer. He took one swig, which seemed to be too much for his thin build and average height. His body stiffened, his eyes popped wide open and he tried to say something. Nothing came out of his mouth but a gurgling peep. He promptly lost his balance and fell to the floor, cushioned by those standing near him. Then we heard the unmistakable sound of a man who had lost all control of his bodily functions. Poor John practically soiled the entire lower part of his uniform, from back to front.

We were laughing so hard – we could not contain ourselves any longer and then John began singing aloud. His high-pitched voice sounded like a girl in distress. We picked him up from the floor and carried him to the nearest bathroom. Someone had filled the bathtub and we unceremoniously dropped him into the cold water without removing his soiled uniform.

On the work front, we were ordered new directives, which were more political than military. It concerned the so-called Automatic Arrest Category. This required us to track down and arrest all members of the Nazi hierarchy, from the leaders of the Hitler Youth, to the SS, security service, Gestapo, and all political party leaders. Martin Bormann, an official of the Nazi Party and head of the Nazi Party Chancellery, had disappeared and was rumored to be hiding in castles, farms and estates all over Germany.

When we received intelligence that he was going to be attending an opera at the local opera house, we staged a raid during the performance. It created a nightmare of indescribable confusion and panic, but in the end he was nowhere to be found.

After a time, we were hot on the trail of Bormann once more when an informant led us to a farm, which we raided in the middle of night. When we kicked the door open, a young man clad only in pants began ringing a large copper bell to warn the others. The sound startled the hell out of me.

Our agents had their pistols drawn, and I had my carbine with the safety off, ready for fire. As we started running with my finger on trigger, I accidentally pulled it and nearly shot my left foot. We conducted many other searches; both in uniform and in civilian clothes, which turned out to be fruitless, so eventually we gave up and focused on other assignments.

Unconditional Surrender

During daylight on May 8, 1945, I was riding in our jeep in Nuremberg with Ray Lustig at the wheel when a C-47 flew over at a very low altitude dropping little balls of red and green fireworks in the sky. We didn't know what to make of it, but we found out by listening to the radio that the war in Europe had come to an end; Germany had surrendered unconditionally, which the Allied forces had demanded. Unlike the major cities throughout the world that took to the streets to rejoice, our outfit did not celebrate at all. While we were happy the war was finally over, it had been a long time coming. In fact, some soldiers were concerned that they would be transferred to the South Pacific to continue the fight against Japan.

It had come to pass that Allied civilian and military personnel were no longer allowed to speak to or associate with German nationals. This was considered fraternization with the enemy and was forbidden by an order issued by SHAEF (Eisenhower's Supreme Headquarters Allied Expedition Forces). It was a directive that unpopular with the GIs, who could not take their eyes off the pretty German girls, who in turn, could not let their gaze stray from the handsome GIs.

To make matters more difficult, our GIs had the coveted cigarettes, coffee, chocolate, butter, and nylons and other goodies that the German girls had been deprived of for over seven years. Not only were these goods no longer available in wartime Germany, but there was also a major shortage of men. The male population was either off fighting in Russia, were prisoners of war, or dead. Despite this ban, practically the entire U.S. Army was engaged in clandestine activity driven by human nature.

The non-fraternization ban did not apply to our team in the CIC. We needed to work with German informants and investigate suspected Nazis who fell within the Automatic Arrest category – in short we needed them to help us with our work. We also worked with the German police, specifically the *Kriminalpolizei*, who did a lot of investigative work for us as well as the U.S. Army's Military Police. We moved our living quarters out of the 27 Wieland Strasse office and into our new home, a villa in the suburban city of Fürth, a 20 minute drive away. Wieland Strasse became our official CIC office in Nuremberg with all our administrative personnel in place and we each had individual offices.

If a German citizen wanted to speak with us, the two MPs stationed outside would first question them and then send them to my office. They were usually denouncing someone or feeding us information and my German was good enough to understand them. Max Steiner, one of our chief interrogators, who was German-born, was too senior to handle these daily requests. He kept his two secretaries (former Gestapo) busy with all of his assignments. I didn't have the luxury of a secretary, but Max and I were friendly with one another, even if I really knew nothing about his personal life. During this time, we found out that the Germans considered us as the "American Gestapo." We thought it a bizarre comparison.

The road leading to our beautiful four-story villa in Fürth passed the Palace of Justice where the Nuremberg trials were being held. My living quarters were lavishly furnished and housed a typical German hearth, made of porcelain that stretched from the floor to the ceiling. I was thrilled to discover a six-band Lumophone radio, a record player that needed cranking and a whole collection of gramophone records featuring the classics: Bach, Wagner, Mozart, and many others.

I had become good friends with a man named Fred Kelly, an unmarried Southerner from Griffith, Georgia. Fred was another member of our CIC team. He was older than I, maybe late twenties, and very handsome with slightly wavy hair. Occasionally, we would toss a football, baseball or even throw horseshoes. One evening after supper, I left my quarters in Fürth to pick up my Lumophone radio that had stopped working. I had taken it to a Yugoslavian repairman who worked in the "conclave"– the very restricted area where the War Crimes Trials were being held.

Since our unit was in charge of security in the building (in and out traffic of persons and vehicles was enforced by MPs), I was there almost every day. All the MPs at the gates knew me by name and would usually wave me through without questions when they saw me. I had signed out in our log as "going to conclave," and since I was just going to do a quick pick up, I went out of uniform and didn't bother carrying my CIC credentials. I parked my jeep and made my way inside the building and down into the basement to my repairman. While he was busily explaining what repairs he had made to my radio, I heard a very loud, "Soldier!" Confused, I turned to face a tall colonel who had his .45 pistol aimed directly at me screaming.

"You're fraternizing! What's your name? Show me your ID!" I tried very hard to explain who I was and what I was doing there, but the man was visibly drunk and kept yelling that I was in violation of the anti-fraternization ban. I was away from my outfit without a trip-ticket and, to boot, out of uniform. He thought I was an ordinary GI and kept aiming his .45 pistol at me, summoning two MPs and kept screaming: "Arrest this guy and throw him in jail."

The MPs looked and me and made a resigned sign with their eyes. They had to obey his order and placed me under arrest, taking me to the inner court, placing me in an empty cell, and shut the door behind me. They felt bad for me but promised to get word to my headquarters. I was flabbergasted. Before I had any time to think, here I was. I, Jack Boeki, victim of Nazi persecution, was in the same prison with the worst murderers and violators of human rights the world had ever seen: Goering, Keitel, Streicher, Hess, Ribbentrop, and other human animals.

What irony! Never could I have dreamt that anything like this would ever happen to me. I wasn't afraid or worried, but I certainly had no idea what was going to happen next. I lay down on the hard bed and listened to the eerie hollow sounds that permeated the prison: clanking doors, footsteps, and echoes. and soon was asleep. It must have been early morning when my cell door opened. There, standing in the doorway was my dear friend, Special Agent Fred Kelly laughing at me.

"We decided we should probably get you outta here!"

I later found out that our commanding officer, Captain Yarnevich threw the book at the Colonel by reporting him to higher ups as drunk on duty, which resulted in him getting sent back to the United States.

CHAPTER 26

Two Wrongs Don't Make a Right

ONE OF MY assigned duties was conducting interrogations. Most prisoners cowered in front of me and acted like innocent pussycats, trying to flatter me or show spurious respect. I knew better. Previously, if our roles had been reversed, they would have killed me without hesitation, because, in their minds, I was only a rat Jew. It was for that reason I always started interrogation by informing my prisoners that I was a Jew. I then proceeded to lay a heavy leather glove on my desk, explaining that it was not there for protection against the cold. This was, of course, my way of intimidation and scare tactics, which worked in some cases, but not in all.

Among the many war criminals I questioned was an older man the MPs told me was alleged to have killed an American pilot whose airplane was shot down somewhere in Germany. He was incarcerated in the Nuremberg prison and had denied the allegations against him. No one had been successful in getting a confession out of him. This matter had been turned over to us, and I was to further interrogate him. This was nothing new for me. I had interrogated dozens of war criminals and gotten enough evidence against most to either send them to prison for the rest of their lives, have them hanged, or have them executed by firing squad.

The alleged killer of the American pilot now stood in front of my desk. I had so much hatred built up in my body for this individual; I did not allow him to sit. He kept denying the charges and insisted that he was not even close to where the airplane had crashed. The written statements of the two witnesses who had reported this incident was on my desk in front of me. It not only testified that he had shot the pilot through the head but that he repeatedly kicked the dead body. I rapidly lost my patience with him and picked up my glove, ordering him to stand against the wall. I was infuriated. I began to hit him over and over and punched his head into the wall. Then, I hit him hard in the stomach. He cowered, and the expression of fear on his face as he tried to back away from me came into sharp focus. Just then, the door opened and Yarny stuck his head in and shouted at me.

"Jack, you can't do that!"

Under certain circumstances, I must admit, I went too far in the treatment of my prisoners – especially the ones who were active in the concentration camps. It made me so angry that they were so callous and did not have the common decency to see me as a worthy human. The only excuse I had was that I knew firsthand what happened in those camps. The maltreatment of prisoners went far beyond the International Law of the Geneva Convention – or human comprehension.

I slowly started to realize that the fear I was instilling in my prisoners was the very same the Germans had instilled in me; I saw it in their faces. The tables had completely turned. I was suddenly starting to feel that if I continued, I was on my way to becoming no better than the Nazis I hated. Really, there was nothing this poor bastard could do in his position. Of course, I knew Yarny was right. From that moment on, I swore to myself that I would ensure there was at least a four-foot distance between myself and any prisoner. I would never lay a hand on any of the prisoners brought in front of me, no matter what crimes they had committed in the past.

Prisoner of War Camp No. 24

In August 1945, I was ordered to one of the new holding camps, POW Camp No. 24, located near Auerbach in Southern Bavaria, Germany. I worked and lived there for about a week. There, I encountered around

50,000 German prisoners of war held behind barbed wire in several huge enclosures. Our armed MPs guarded them, and my job was to ferret out, interrogate and arrest members of organizations that fell under the Automatic Arrest categories.

In the chaos of Germany's surrender, members of Nazi organizations got rid of their uniforms and changed into civilian clothes because they feared retribution. When they could not find civilian clothes, they removed the insignia from their uniforms to at least hide their rank and organization. Interestingly, civilian SS officials also changed into ordinary soldiers' uniforms because members of the German Army, who became prisoners of war did not have much to fear; the Geneva Convention protected them from punishment. However, members of the SS, both civilian and military, had to account for their crimes.

I had my work cut out for me, and I was well trained for the job. I had attended several study sessions covering the methods Nazis used to evade arrest. I also was armed with lists of known war criminals with a short history of their activities and possible whereabouts. I had to conduct mass interrogations primarily based on intimidation and subterfuge.

There were too many prisoners for me to interrogate one by one, so when I went to work, I was protected by four armed MPs. Standing in front of a camp full of German POWs, I ordered them all to stand at attention while I spoke. I held an impressive red-colored notebook above my head so all could see. Then, in my best authoritative German, I let them know the book contained the names and ranks of all known war criminals in the Automatic Arrest categories established by the International War Crimes Commission in Washington, D.C. I claimed that these documents had been signed off by President Franklin D. Roosevelt – I made this up, of course.

I would stare sharply into the crowd and continue by asking all persons who committed war crimes to step forward. And of course, no one did. I would then ask all members of the Gestapo to step forward, followed by all members of the SS, and so on, until I had made my way through all the Automatic Arrest categories. This procedure intimidated some, and those that stepped forward were arrested by our MPs and led away for further interrogation and possible punishment.

This was phase one of my procedure. I then announced that prisoners who had misled us and were later found to be lying would automatically be turned over to our Russian allies for further questioning. This threat was a total fabrication, but it had amazing results. It caused additional Nazis to step forward because they would rather become prisoners of Americans than be handed over to the Russians, who had a dreaded reputation for treating POWs ruthlessly.

The next step of my intimidation was to call out the names of war criminals that were actually on my list. No one ever stepped forward, and I was never too surprised. I would go through this routine more to make an impression than to immediately catch more fish in my net.

My routine followed with two final steps. In a loud voice, I ordered everyone to empty their pockets and place all contents in front of them – followed by "*gepäck holen*," which meant for them to get whatever packs they had and empty them in front of us. The MPs and I searched through all their stuff, which often produced enough evidence to establish the identity of more Nazis. Unfortunately, we were not able to search each prisoners' effects thoroughly as we didn't have enough manpower.

When those remaining thought they had withstood my interrogation, I would launch into the last phase of my routine. I told them I had dutifully followed my orders to seek out people facing arrest and had reason to believe that there were still war criminals, Gestapo agents and members of the SS hiding amongst them. These criminals were guilty of everything from rape to murder and other atrocities that stunned the civilized world. It would be their last chance to come forward and avoid being turned over to the Russians.

That was effective and yielded results, but it was only a prelude to the last stroke of genius: ordering everyone to remove their shirts and undershirts. I believe this caught most of them off guard, and they stood there, perhaps a bit embarrassed, with their chests bare. Now I directed them to raise their arms high and keep them there. This ploy produced amazing results as Waffen-SS members had a small black tattoo on the inner side of their upper left arm, closest to their armpit.

The tattoos indicated their blood type in case they required a blood transfusion while injured and rendered unconscious. We would walk through the ranks of bare-chested prisoners with their arms raised and could easily identify the tattoos. Some had already planned ahead and had their tattoos removed; however, we could still detect a fresh scar where the tattoo used to be. These types would give us the excuse that they had been wounded during combat, but we knew better. It filled me with such fury to stand nose-to-nose and eye-to-eye with people who were capable of inflicting such torture, cruelty and death.

One day I discovered a Ukrainian man who was short and had a face like a hyena. I had him step forward separately and, when he did so, I could smell his filthy body; he probably had not washed for many days. At first, I asked him the usual questions.

"Name; rank or profession; where born; nationality." His replies, uttered in his high-pitched annoying voice, were not unusual. But when I came to the last question, "Where served," this human animal mentioned the name of a camp that I had never heard of. He had been a guard, they called a *Kapo*. This type of criminal was known to be extremely cruel to Jews; many had actively participated in killings. I asked if there had been any Jews in that camp and he confirmed with a nod.

"How many Jews did you kill?" shot out of my mouth, completely unexpected. He just shrugged his shoulders.

At that point, I completely lost my senses. To be so flippant about the lives of so many innocents flipped a switch inside of me. My anger came to a full boil. I was so enraged. I don't know what happened – I just started beating him. By the time I was done, he had landed on the ground and lay there gasping. I'm not sure how it happened, but I went completely against my vow to never use violence against another prisoner.

The commanding officer of the POW camp received reports about this incident and called me into his office. He began with a stern lecture: He would not tolerate the mistreatment of prisoners under his watch. I was to interview POWs, create their reports and nothing more. I had to leave it up to the others to determine the appropriate punishment.

I had acted completely out of line, and he would not hesitate to throw the book at me – and I knew that meant I could be court-martialed.

I was getting raked over the coals and admitted to overstepping the rules. I felt I had to explain that I completely lost my cool when the prisoner admitted to having been a concentration camp guard. I tried to explain to my superior that these were the same bastards who had been after me when I lived in Holland and hid out in France. They might have been successful in murdering me were it not for sheer luck. God only knows what fate they may have bestowed on my family! That man and his kind were responsible for everything I and the Jewish people of Europe had gone through.

The commanding officer had not been aware of my background, but my explanation seemed to pacify him. The matter was dropped, and I was fortunate enough to never face any further repercussions. At first I felt horrible, and then I didn't; processing war criminals was hard to reconcile. Working at the POW camp left me exhausted. I shouted orders all day long, and by evening, I had hardly any voice left. It was a psychological challenge as well as a physical and emotional one, not to mention the paperwork. Reports that recounted my activities for the day:

ARRESTED

- 1 war criminal
- 3 Gestapo agents
- 305 members of the Waffen-SS
- 5 members of Allgemeine-SS
- 2 Kapos

Despite the strain, the work had a distinct benefit for me; it relieved some of my trauma because it gave me the chance to ensure justice was served and to feel somewhat avenged. There was the hope for some form of accountability.

The Von Stauffenberg Affair — Fall 1945

I was happy to be back in Nuremberg. One day, while I was handling the reception area, a tall attractive woman was ushered into my office. She was introduced as the Countess von Stauffenberg. She explained that her husband, Count Claus von Stauffenberg, was the person who had placed the bomb under Hitler's conference table. Stauffenberg, an aristocratic colonel and handsome man, lost his right hand and wore an eye patch after being wounded fighting with Rommel in North Africa. He took on the risky work of assassinating Hitler himself, stashing his bomb-laden briefcase near the Führer as he held court with military strategists at his headquarters in East Prussia (now Poland). The bomb killed five people but missed its target, wounding Hitler only slightly.

Her husband was shot and killed as a traitor, and all their family possessions and real-estate holdings were confiscated. This included their castle, which resulted in her family becoming homeless once she was out of prison. She came to us to seek our help in finding the family heirlooms that had been confiscated by the Gestapo. The whole world knew of the failed plot to kill Hitler, but I had never heard the name Von Stauffenberg before. I wrote a short report of her visit and request, but my commanding officer, Yarny, told me that this was not a matter of counterintelligence and should be turned over to the Military Government.

A few months later, several suitcases were discovered in the basement of a bank by one of our teams led by Special Agent Grover Cordts. When they arrived and were opened in our office, they were found to contain rare gems, gold and platinum jewelry, ornaments, and silver flatware monogrammed with the Von Stauffenberg name. We all gaped at that treasure trove; most of us had never seen such an array of valuables representing a small fortune. The find was turned over to Military Government officials who would then turn it over to its rightful owner, the widow Von Stauffenberg.

CHAPTER 27

Furlough to Holland

In December 1945, I requested a two-week furlough to travel to Holland to straighten out my citizenship and necessary documentation required by the American government, as I wanted to become an American citizen. The leave was granted by our second in command, Special Agent John Slater and authorized travel was by motor transport. I didn't want to drive alone in a jeep for a trip of about 600 kilometers, so I asked my buddy Leo Tryk if he would like to come along.

Leo was happy to travel with me, and he arranged for a furlough and travel documents. We loaded up our jeep with plenty of gas, K-rations and personal belongings. We took off one early morning, reaching the city of Venlo in Holland by early evening. We needed to find a place to sleep. We were tired after driving the whole day and found a military encampment stationed there. It was the Jewish Brigade (the Jews from Palestine who had volunteered to fight in the war and became part of the British Army). The commanding officer received us warmly, invited us to dinner and put us up for the night in one of their tents.

When we reached Rotterdam, the first thing I did was look up Esther; I still remembered her address. Her brother, Bram answered the door and there I stood in full uniform, which must have made quite an impression. I was taken by surprise when he told me Esther did not want to see me. I did not insist; I turned my back and carried on.

Next, I went to look up the only person who might know the whereabouts of my family: my childhood nanny Sienne, who was still close to my heart. My parents employed her as our housekeeper before the German invasion of Holland, and her husband, Jan, worked for my father's many stores as a handyman. Her son, Bas, also worked for my father and his wife, Stien, a schoolteacher, was the sister of Bets, who was Big Harry's mother.

I was excited when I rang the doorbell at their residence. Our jeep was parked out front and in a short time had collected a throng of admirers who were shouting, "Look, Americans! Americans! Welcome – welcome!"

Many looked at Tryk and me as if we came from another planet, and some even tried to touch us. They were thanking us for liberating them when Sienne answered the door. She had quickly come down from the top of a steep staircase when she heard the noise of the people yelling and saw the commotion in front of her door. Her mouth fell open when she spotted me. With tears in her eyes, she flew at me, embracing me, unable to utter a word. In short order, Jan also came down, followed by Bas and his wife, who both lived on the second floor. They couldn't believe their eyes, taking in what was happening in front of their door: the crowd, the yelling, the jeep, and in the middle of the turmoil – two American soldiers. Their eyes were focused on me.

Looking at each other with big eyes, "Is it him? Could this be, Shjakie Boeki? It looks like him!"

Bewildered and unbelieving, they approached me and finally recognized me. It was a joyful and utterly happy event for everybody. Tryk and I went upstairs, and Sienne made us something to eat and insisted we spend the night with them. She wanted us to sleep in her bed, changed the sheets, and would not take no for an answer. We stayed the entire next day with the whole family. They wanted to hear how I had survived and how I got into the American Army.

Poor Tryk didn't understand a word of Dutch, so I occasionally filled him in on the conversation. The entire family didn't know anything about my parents and sisters. They didn't expect them to have survived. People had been picked up by the police and completely disappeared without a trace. Based on what I had witnessed and what was in the newspapers, I also did not expect to find them alive – but I still didn't know for sure. I thanked Sienne and her family for their hospitality, and Tryk and I moved into a hotel.

Tryk and I had a wonderful time. Everywhere we went, people admired us and thanked us for the liberation from the hated German occupation. Bas told me that he had to go to Amsterdam, so I drove him in the jeep. There, we almost caused a riot; so many people surrounded us who had never seen American soldiers. They treated us as if we were Hollywood movie stars.

I had to get started with my official paperwork. When I presented myself to the municipal offices to get my birth certificate and proof of citizenship, I was told that I needed a witness who could vouch that I was Jack Isaac Boeki, son of Jacob and Leentje Boeki – Berkelouw. Bas helped me out with this. I received the birth certificate, but to my surprise, the citizenship document stated I was a Dutch citizen "until March 13, 1943, when his name was removed from the municipal register as 'whereabouts unknown.'" This left me without a passport and, to an extent, stateless. I went as far as I could go at this point and we headed back to Nuremberg.

The Dutch Captain

In civilian life, the majority of members in our detachment were lawyers, college professors or officers of government law-enforcement agencies, all in their late thirties and early forties. These men were my colleagues, friends and close mentors. In some cases they even acted like father figures. We enjoyed a lot of ribbing and jokes amongst us to ease the heaviness of the war, and as I was the youngest, only 22 at the time, I seemed to get the brunt of it. We often laughed at ourselves being CIC agents, saying the letters stood for "Christ, I'm Confused."

Everyone liked Don McClure, who was never in a hurry and always had a smile on his face. He was known as an adorable fellow who was "pleasantly" plump, blondish with a moustache and always spoke slowly and succinctly. In civilian life, Don was a treasury agent for the U.S.

government. On a trip we took to Munich together, we made time to stop, taking many photos along the way.

Earl Randall must've been in his late thirties and had been a college professor who spoke several languages, including Dutch. Lanky with blondish hair, he was a reserved man who looked like a typical academic. I can't remember when I first met him, but it was somewhere in France during combat. After I had been transferred from a previous location, I was sitting next to him at a makeshift breakfast table when he asked me in fluent Dutch if I liked pancakes. I was dumbfounded.

He was married to a Dutch woman and had picked up the language from her. Of course, we became friends afterwards and I had great respect for him. He had a high security clearance and was our chief interrogator, investigating war criminals like Julius Streicher.

One particular day, I walked in unexpectedly during one of Julius Streicher's interrogation sessions (I wasn't supposed to be there). It was a small room where Earl was questioning him. Streicher was a stubborn and arrogant Nazi who looked like a bully. I asked him how many Jews he had killed, thinking he personally had a hand in this – his answer was that he did not participate in any killings, but "only wrote informative articles." He said that he was on trial for "simply writing words." Born in 1885, he ended up as the editor of the Nazi newspaper, *Der Stürmer*, whose sole purpose was to create a deep hatred for the Jewish people. He had been captured at the end of the war and brought to Nuremberg, where three members of our team interrogated him. While awaiting sentencing, guards continuously watched him, peering through the opening in his cell door. In fact, this was done to keep an eye on all the war crimes prisoners.

One Sunday, I was having breakfast in our large dining room that could seat at least 20 people. It seemed on that particular Sunday, all or most of our agents were present, which was not always the case. Many slept in or skipped breakfast because for most of us, Sunday was our day off duty. This was also the day visitors and guests were invited, so it was not surprising that an officer dressed in a uniform I couldn't identify walked in and took a seat next to our commander Ernest Yarnevich. Shortly thereafter, Yarny called me over and introduced me to Captain Smit of the Royal Dutch Army, who immediately started speaking to me in Dutch. I had become used to an attitude that anything foreign was substandard and un-American; therefore speaking Dutch now embarrassed me.

He asked where I was born and my age, and continued in a strict, official tone explaining that as a Dutch citizen, I was to report to him in the morning to be inducted into the Royal Dutch Army. Holland was still at war with Japan and needed to call on its citizens. My breathing stopped short, and I felt the blood draining from my head. I looked at Yarny, who had a serious look on his face and said he had tried everything but couldn't stop the Dutch government from conscripting me. The technical difficulty was that I was still legally a Dutch citizen. I protested stating that I had my duties to carry out in the U.S. Army and they couldn't do this to me. I did not want to go to Holland, let alone join their army.

The Dutch captain interjected and made sure it was clear that if I resisted, I would be considered a deserter and would end up in a Dutch prison for sure. My world came to an end. With begging eyes, I looked at the others. Everyone looked stern.

"Listen Jack, you have to serve your country, just like we're serving ours." On and on went the remarks of encouragement around the table.

"Too bad, Jack, we'll miss you." they kept repeating.

Someone suddenly burst out laughing. Apparently they couldn't control themselves any longer and the others all joined in. The laughing continued for a while, with me looking around flabbergasted. Only then did I realize this had been a very cleverly orchestrated prank that I fell for – hook, line and sinker. They had succeeded in scaring me out of my wits. The Dutch captain turned out to be Frank Willis from New York, who was an FBI agent. Weeks later I still kept getting teased.

"Hey, Jack. That Dutch captain is still looking for you!"

CHAPTER 28

Inge — Bad Homburg

IN THE FALL of 1946, after my assignments in Nuremberg and Camp Auerbach, things began to change. Most of the CIC agents on my team had accumulated enough service points to be eligible for discharge and a return to the States. I had enough points as well, but I was afraid to return to the U.S., where I knew practically no one and where labor strikes and unrest were taking place. So, I signed up for another year and was transferred to Bad Homburg, some 30 kilometers from Frankfurt am Main.

I had come to love life in the army called the "ETO" (The European Theater of Operations). It became my father and mother; it gave me a home, food, shelter and security, which I needed as a young man whose youth had been taken away by the German invasion.

Instead of being assigned to a field office, the CIC put me up in the Hotel Minerva, a palatial hotel on a hill overlooking a breathtaking park that housed the famous Kaiser Wilhelm Kurhaus, where European aristocracy and the very rich came to enjoy the medicinal spring waters. This spa treatment center looked more like a marble palace than anything else. The surroundings were breathtaking: lush green lawns and tall oak trees lined most of the avenues and in the far distance, the Taunus Mountains peaked high above the horizon. Various wells throughout the park were fashioned so that the effervescent waters flowed from a tap, enabling people to drink from it.

No wonder the army brass found housing for the Supreme Commander of the Army, General Dwight D. Eisenhower, not far from our hotel. His was an estate built on the edge of a ravine and surrounded by an honor guard of highly decorated members of the 101st and 82nd Airborne Divisions in full-dress uniform with chrome-plated helmets. It was quite a sight seeing him leave early in the morning on his way to Frankfurt, which was SHAEF Headquarters.

Our hotel was not used for intelligence purposes but accommodated transient agents and personnel from the intelligence center in Oberursel either on their way back to the States or to duties elsewhere. I had the good fortune of running into Ray Lustig after his discharge, on his way back home. It really hit me that I was losing track of my team, which had felt like home to me.

There was little for me to do here, and I became bored. Robert Mann, or Bob, was from Erie, Pennsylvania, and was around my age. He was not a CIC agent, but was in charge of the food and liquor supply for the Hotel Minerva. We hung out a lot together, playing a lot of ping-pong. Since I didn't have much to do, I frequently accompanied him to an army supply center to pick up liquor. He told me his father owned a funeral home and he had been studying to be an undertaker when he was drafted.

Then one day strolling in front of my hotel, I saw a beautiful woman. My "hello" was answered in fluent English. She explained she was on her way to the Charlie Ritter Park Tennis Club to meet some friends. She invited me to come along, which I gladly accepted. Her name was Inge Schmidt, a married beauty. She had two children: a girl named Leila, aged four and a baby boy, whom she called "*brüderchen*," or little brother. The Russians were holding her husband, an officer in the German army, as a POW. Slender, long-limbed, with shoulder-length blonde hair, a Germanic face and steel-blue eyes. These eyes pierced me, as if she were firing a hot metal arrow into my heart.

I was 22 years old and fell hopelessly in love with this girl who was four years older than I, yet looked like a teenager. We had a strong mutual attraction but had nothing in common outside of sex, drinking Mosel wine and partying. Her apartment was not far from my hotel, where I stayed more often than not. Occasionally she had her two children there, but she generally kept them permanently at the childcare center, as she said they hampered our activities.

Then orders came through sending me to Berlin for a temporary assignment. This was to supervise security clearances for 500 German nationals who had applied to work for the U.S. Army. All these people needed to be investigated and fingerprinted prior to being hired. I wanted this job done as fast as possible to return to Inge in the shortest possible time. After a three-week-absence, I was back in Bad Homburg, where she was impatiently waiting.

Our worry-free lifestyle continued. I got into trouble at one particular drinking party. I was challenged to drink a full glass of alcohol in one gulp. The glass contained a mixture of whiskey, gin, rum and beer. Stupidly, I emptied the whole glass, whereupon I promptly blacked out. I cannot remember what happened that night. But the next day, I found out I had beaten up a British soldier so badly that he had to be hospitalized. I had absolutely no recollection of having done this, or the reason for it. I felt remorseful and went to the hospital to offer my apologies. It was obvious I couldn't handle alcohol, as I'm not someone who drinks.

Then, a month or so after I had completed my Berlin assignment, I received new orders to proceed to Bremerhaven to join the CIC field office there. This was not only a city far away from Bad Homburg, but the assignment was a permanent one. I failed to get the orders changed and prepared to leave for Bremerhaven. I told Inge not to worry. I had enough buddies in the Air Force to get rides to enable me to see her at least one weekend per month. That was the best I could do under the circumstances. We said our sad goodbyes, and I went on my way with a funny feeling in my stomach.

Bremerhaven is a port in northern Germany bounded by the city of Bremen. When I arrived, the first thing I noticed was its strong smell of fish. The CIC offices were in an apartment instead of the luxurious villas or estates the CIC usually occupied. I instantly disliked everything around me. Compared to beautiful Bad Homburg, this place was a real dump. On top of that, being away from Inge made me lovesick. I had difficulty concentrating on my work, and my commanding officer was not happy with my performance. I could no longer sleep or eat. My condition got worse by the day. My teammates tried to cheer me up and even introduced me to several WACs (Women Army Corps personnel), but I was totally uninterested.

I applied for a transfer back to Bad Homburg and my commanding officer was happy to oblige. However, it took three months for the transfer to come through. When I arrived in Bad Homburg after a tedious train ride, I rushed to Inge's apartment instead of reporting to the Hotel Minerva, only to find Inge away.

The neighbors told me she had been away for several days, which she had frequently done during my absence. Disappointed, I went to my hotel, reported in and unpacked my bags. My friend Bob was still on duty at the hotel and told me to shape up and not worry so much about Inge.

"In fact," he said, "I don't think she's very serious about you, because I bedded her, too". My heart stood still. I acted as if it did not mean much to me, but it felt like my insides were being pulled out. Unfortunately, this was not enough of a warning for lovesick me.

When she finally returned from wherever she had been, I confronted her. She denied everything my friend had told me, and I was only too happy to believe her. At that time, I would have believed anything because I was completely blinded by my passion and love for her.

Life went on, and to keep myself busy, I discovered a completely equipped dark room with the latest U.S. Army photographic technology in the hotel's basement. I began developing and printing my own photos. Others found out what I was doing and soon I had my hands full helping them with their pictures. Other than that, I was at Inge's place most of the time.

Our madness continued until she became pregnant. An abortion was considered too dangerous by her doctor, and I felt the honorable thing to do was to marry her. However, the U.S. Army forbade marriage to German nationals. The easiest and fastest thing for me was to get my discharge in Germany instead of in the U.S. Thus, I applied for a discharge, which was soon granted.

Inge obtained a quick divorce from her husband, I had become a civilian and we were married by a city official at the Bad Homburg City Hall. With the benefit of hindsight, while this was probably a noble thing to do, it was not a very wise move on my part, having given up my official army career. I was young, in love, totally blind and naïve. In August 1947, a baby boy was born whom we called Allan.

I applied for a job with the Army Post Exchange (PX) Service, which was in dire need of security personnel. When they read my service records and realized I was a former CIC agent, they immediately employed me as a security investigator. I discovered a host of security leaks at the vast army depots in Schierstein, where the PX maintained huge inventories to supply the various offices throughout the U.S. zone of occupation.

I moved out of the Hotel Minerva and transferred to billets in Schierstein, not far from the beautiful city of Wiesbaden. Inge stayed in Bad Homburg, since she was not allowed to live with me on army installations. I could only be with her over weekends, when I traveled from Schierstein to Bad Homburg – a distance of roughly one hour by jeep.

I worked in Schierstein for one year, until when my contract was up. I decided not to renew it so that I could relocate my family to Holland. I was now a married man with three children. My intention was to petition the Dutch authorities to let my German wife and three children immigrate to Holland.

I arrived in Holland alone in the dead of winter in February 1948 to set things up. The police were still wearing the same uniforms as during the German occupation, and every time I spotted one, I felt like killing them. I was staying in a rooming house in Rotterdam that Big Harry helped me find. I had seen the results of the barbaric mass extermination of the European Jews in Germany and had little hope my parents had escaped the horror. I didn't know what happened to my family until I received official information from the Red Cross that my father Jacob, my mother Leentje, and my sister Lea were transported in April 1943 to Camp Westerbork, from where they were deported to the death camp, Sobibor in Poland and murdered by gas upon arrival on April 30, 1943.

I also received a letter from the man who had been the underground contact who placed us with the different families in Ede. He explained that my parents' hiding place was betrayed and they were arrested. The thing that breaks my heart is that somehow, my sister Lea, who was safe and hiding in a different location, found out about my parents' arrest and insisted on joining them. I often think my younger sister, Lea might have survived if she did not willingly join my parents. Our hiding place in Ede was the last time I saw them. I could not get this out of my mind.

My older sister Hannah, her husband Isidor, and their three children – the oldest Appie, age 12; Little Lea, age 4; and the baby Sylvia, age 6 months – met the same fate a month later. This news did not surprise me, but at least I got confirmation about what happened to them. All my uncles, aunts, cousins, nephews and friends were all murdered in different concentration camps, making me the sole survivor of my family.

Holland was a constant reminder that my entire family had been erased. It was dreary and depressing, and I felt like a stranger in my own country. However, I still went through with contacting the proper authorities to begin the process of relocating my new family. After many weeks of frustrating interviews, it became clear to me that bringing them to the Netherlands was an impossibility. A country that was plundered and raped by the Germans was not ready to invite German nationals in. I got into several fistfights because I kept encountering racial insults. I felt desperate, lonely, and depressed.

On an impulse, I returned to Bad Homburg intending to surprise Inge. I had to enter Germany illegally because it was still an occupied country. When I arrived at Inge's apartment she was not home. The neighbors told me she was frequently seen with "an American officer, who had stayed overnight with her." She had left a few days ago with the same officer, who had picked her up in his car. Despite everything, I let myself into the apartment and waited three days at the window, peering into the street, before she finally showed up. An army staff car stopped in front of the apartment. Inge kissed the officer behind the wheel and stepped out.

My world ended. In my mind, I saw buildings crumbling and disappearing into the earth. The floor under my feet started swaying and I felt nauseous. When I confronted her about her indiscretion, things became extremely heated. I was deeply hurt and that injury turned to anger. I started screaming at her and when I regained control over myself, I didn't say a word. I took one last look at her, opened the door and left, never to return. I did not answer her phone calls nor her letters. She was dead to me.

PART V

AFTER THE WAR

CHAPTER 29

Life in Holland

ALONG EVERY MILE of railroad track on my way back to Holland, I was distressed and heartbroken about the breakup with Inge. Despite this, I didn't want anything more to do with her. It had been more than enough for me. After I had settled in and found a place to live in Rotterdam, I received several letters from her. I returned them unopened and started the long complex process of obtaining an international divorce. It took three years before it finally came through.

Meanwhile, there I was, back in my old hometown. It didn't feel like home. I felt like a visitor in a strange city. Many things looked familiar but created a mixed feeling of sadness, joy and longing. I was totally unhappy and lonely.

The weather was cold and blustery; everything looked bleak. Happy childhood memories were overshadowed by recalling how my home was bombed and how the Germans and their Dutch cohorts had hunted and chased me through the streets, shot at me, threw me into prison and murdered my family. I lived in different rooming houses and hated every one of them.

Eventually, I got in touch with my cousin, Big Harry. As it turned out, he was the only other member of our family who had survived the Holocaust. His mother was not Jewish, and she testified in court that her husband (a Jew) was not the father of her son. The Nazis believed her, and she got away with it. It made my cousin, Harry, a non-Jew, which saved his life.

He was good to me and helped me in many ways. At the time, Harry was married and lived in a nice apartment. They had an Airedale Terrier that I used to play-fight with. I loved that dog so much. Harry introduced me to the ways of business – selling and making money. I knew nothing about these things and didn't like it too much. We formed a company that I named "Esquistia." It was a business selling ladies' hats to various millinery stores.

Harry had made a deal with a manufacturer of ladies' hats to purchase their merchandise at wholesale prices that we pre-sold to stores for a profit. The manufacturer supplied us with sample hats. In order to retain the delicate shape of the samples, the manufacturer had designed sample cases to carry them in for presentation to the buyers.

These huge, black-colored monstrosities looked more like coffins than sample cases. They were so wide and high that I had to carry them away from my body which was very unkind to my arms. After an arduous walk of only five minutes, both my arms would cramp up. This was definitely not ideal for a sales presentation. I first had to put the cases down to open the entrance doors, then I had to jam my foot in the door in an effort to keep it open. After, I had to pick up one case at a time and shove them individually through the door. By the time both sample cases were inside the store, I was out of breath with two lame arms. The storekeepers always watched this whole exercise with mouths agape.

I never made a sale in the short time I allowed myself to do this kind of work. Then, one day I walked into a clothing store and the storekeeper didn't allow me to make a presentation because, he said, "I don't do business with Jews."

"What?" I said. Then I punched him so hard in the jaw that he fell backwards, smashing into the mirror – it was one of those tall swivel mirrors for customers to check the fit of their clothes. Fortunately for both of us, he only incurred a few cuts and scratches, but it could have killed him. The repercussions for me were minor. When the police came and I told them what he had said to start the fracas, they understood, and I never heard anything further about it.

This was the straw that broke the camel's back. I had had more than enough and told Harry I didn't like what I was doing. The only thing he did was drive me around to the various stores and stay in the car. I didn't care about the money I had invested and told Harry to shove it.

I remained deeply unhappy in Rotterdam. I had no friends or family; everyone had been murdered. I had alienated Harry – the only family I had left. I had even gotten into an argument with Sienne's family over items they had removed from my parents' apartment. I lost out on war-damages compensation for those items because they were unaccounted for. In the end, I felt bad for getting upset with them.

I felt alone. The feeling overpowered me. I no longer saw familiar faces in my neighborhood; everyone was gone and I obviously did not fit in. People laughed at me, saying, "Look at this guy, he doesn't know how to dress. He wears his shirt over his pants and his colors don't match." I wore clothes I had bought by mail-order from Sears-Roebuck in Chicago, while in the army, so people thought I was some crazy American.

People were right; while in the U.S. Army, I had become like an American. I didn't fit into the scene in Holland. I couldn't find cornflakes, orange juice, or anything I liked in the grocery stores. Even eating breakfast out was difficult, there were no restaurants open early enough in the morning. When I finally found one open, the waitress looked at me strangely when I tried to order pancakes.

"Pancakes, in the morning? Who ever heard of that?" Whatever was available in restaurants was food I did not like. The irritations were endless. One morning, I was shaving when my landlady knocked on my door. With a broad gesture she said, "There is someone here who wants to talk to you." Annoyed, I looked behind her. A scrawny individual appeared, looking sternly at me, and bowled me over with his question: "Do you own an electric razor?"

"Sure," I said, even more annoyed. "Why?"

He explained he was from the *Storingsdienst*. Believe it or not, the Dutch had an official government agency charged with ferreting out radio static.

"The neighbors have been complaining about you," he reported. "You're interfering with their radio reception. You have to stop using that razor."

It took a couple of seconds for all that to sink in. Then comprehension took effect and I responded with a series of American insults only a guy with years of experience in the U.S. Army would recognize. I don't know whether he grasped the insult, but he got my message: exactly what he could do with his silly noise detector and where to put it.

The Hague

I HAD TO get away from my miserable existence in Rotterdam, so I moved further north to The Hague. It was a beautiful, clean, well-maintained city, home to the Queen and the government. There I was happier, especially after I met a pre-war friend, Harry Fransman, who had survived Auschwitz. He looked very much like me – same wavy hair, same build – but was just a bit older. His father was a well-known pastry chef who had a bakery in The Hague. We got along well and decided to rent an apartment together.

It was early spring, and I was glad the people I met in The Hague were infinitely friendlier than the ones in Rotterdam. Rather than seeing me as an American nutcase, my new friends regarded me as an American hero. They invited me to parties where men slapped my back and girls adored me. They thought my American clothing was snazzy, especially my penny-loafers.

They were eager for anything American, and so was I. Whenever I spotted Americans visiting Holland, I offered directions or anything to start a conversation. I just wanted to be near Americans and speak "American." Being used to American food, I was always on the lookout for some. One day, I passed a grocery store featuring baskets full of multicolored ears of corn.

"Ha!" I said to myself, "Finally I can cook up some corn like they served in the army!"

I bought a dozen ears and hurried to my apartment. I proudly showed off my newfound treasure to my friends and promised, "Now I'll treat you to a real American delicacy." The trouble was, I had never prepared fresh corn, nor had I ever even seen whole ears of corn before. The corn I ate in the army came from cans. I just assumed the corn I had bought had to be boiled, probably for quite a long time, because the ears felt hard to the touch.

After boiling them for 20 minutes, they still were hard as a rock. After 40 minutes, they were no softer. I couldn't believe American housewives had to wait so long to get corn ready for the table, but I left the pot on the fire the whole afternoon, and my supposedly delicious corn still was inedible. Irritated and embarrassed in front of my friends, I returned to the store to complain.

"Cooking?" said the man behind the counter. "What for, cooking? You don't eat that stuff – you use it for fall decorations on your front door. Corn is not food, except for pigs." That is how I learned there are different kinds of corn.

In The Hague, I still had money to live on from what I had earned in Germany, but eventually, I had to start making a living again. I found work at Nolex, a branch of the Borneo Sumatra Trading Company, the successor to the Dutch East Indies Trading Company. They were a global company with about 200 offices that sold everything from locomotives to peanuts. They sent me to their Hong Kong office for a six-month training period. I was excited at the change of scenery and glad to get away from Holland.

Being in Hong Kong was electrifying. I learned a lot about international trading, gained import and export expertise, and mastered how to eat with chopsticks. I fell in love with authentic Chinese food, and women. After the training was over, the company wanted me back at their main office in The Hague. I tried to persuade them to keep me in Asia, but they refused.

In The Hague, I became increasingly miserable, largely because my office was full of stuffy Dutch men who acted jealous of my success and made fun of me. The girls in the office were different. They all took a liking to me, and of course, the priggish gents noticed this and hated me all the more for it. I told them all to go to hell and quit my job.

I was an unhappy man again, and my actions reflected my bad moods. One day, I went through a red traffic light while riding a bike. A traffic cop happened to notice, grabbed me by the shoulder, and dragged me off my bike. I hadn't realized I had done anything wrong. I had been in deep thought and, upon feeling his hands on my shoulder, I exploded into a torrent of Army insults and curses. Fortunately, the cop did not understand any of it. Even if he had understood me, I wouldn't have cared anyway.

Luckily, a bystander who had witnessed the incident understood English and came to my aid. He made up a wonderful excuse.

"This guy is an American from the Embassy." He said, "You'd better let him go if you don't want to get involved in an international diplomatic incident." Phew! That let me off the hook.

The BORSUMY Trading Company rehired me to handle international sales and English communications. I became friendly with my new manager, Anthony Peek. He and his wife, Mia, invited me to move into their home and took good care of me. They also were tired of life in Holland and started to make plans to emigrate to Australia. They wanted me to go with them and help start a business there. I was uncertain. Australia was very far away both Holland and America, which always had a special place in my heart.

Still, I was tempted to go with them, and this showed up in a recurring dream. I saw myself about to board a ship bound for Australia, but I had not packed my bags yet. I also couldn't find my passport, so the ship sailed off without me. The dream was like a premonition. Tony and Mia left Holland, but I stayed behind. They corresponded with me for a long time, urging me to join them in Australia, but I never did.

There was a social club called The International Club, which only admitted U.S. Army personnel and members of the diplomatic corps. I was walking nearby when I saw Sergeant Clinton Brake whom I had met in Germany. We recognized each other immediately and he invited me into the club, where we had some drinks and shared memories. It turned out he was a security guard at the American Embassy, what a happy coincidence!

Eventually, I started to forget the debacle with Inge and went looking for other female company. There was a hangout in The Hague called The Palm Hut, which was always packed with attractive young people, and I liked the music and the dancing. It was 1949, and there was a law restricting folks below the age of 18 from entering this kind of establishment. It had nothing to do with the use of alcohol, because it wasn't served there. It had more to do with the local sense of morality.

One evening while I was there, the police conducted a raid. I've always looked young for my age, and the police ignored my protests that I was well over 18. They shoved me into their van right along with much younger people. The van was overloaded. Many of us had to stand, and when it swerved, a cute girl fell against me. Her face looked pretty, but worried. From the conversation I had overheard between her and a girlfriend, I realized she was afraid of what would happen to her.

"I think my parents will kill me if they hear about this," I had heard her say.

So I said, "Don't worry about the police. We'll just tell them that you're with me and that I'm responsible for you. I have ID showing I'm over 18. They'll probably let you go and won't notify your parents."

The ploy worked well. They let her go, and Mary, the pretty girl, gave me a little kiss on the cheek in gratitude and also her address. She suggested I drop by and meet her parents. I rehearsed her name, Mary de Zoete, so I wouldn't forget it. And I actually didn't forget her it, but I wrote her off as too young and I lost the piece of paper on which I had scribbled her address.

I came across it later and one evening, when I had nothing better to do, I went to that address. There I met her parents, as Mary had suggested. They immediately took to me. Her mother told me that Mary repeatedly had asked if I had called, and acted disappointed about not hearing from me. When she came home and saw me there, she was delighted. With the blessings of her parents, I took her to the movies and thus began our love affair. She was 18 going on 19, while I was 25.

Mary was sweet and angelic. We soon became an item. She had a lovely family. Her mother, Siska, treated me as if I was her own son. She was a great cook and we would play cards while I ate the delicious eggs and bread with thick butter. Her father, Piet, was kind and had great respect for me. Their own son was serving in the Dutch Navy on an aircraft carrier named *Karel Doorman*.

The Baseball That Changed My Destiny

I still missed America and anything American – the food, the people. I didn't like many of the Dutch people around me, with the exception of my friends whom I chose carefully. I hung out a lot with Clint, Harry Cook and other personnel and security officers from the American Embassy. One day, I was playing baseball with a group of them on the beach near The Hague when the ball got away from me. I ran after it, and it rolled right next to a young woman, who looked up at me.

"Sorry," I said.

"Are you American?" she asked.

"More or less," I laughed and ran back to my friends.

When our game was over and we sat on the sand, the young woman approached us and started talking in perfect English, explaining that right after the war, she worked for the UNRRA, the United Nations Relief and Rehabilitation Administration, a U.S.-sponsored organization that helped displaced victims of the Nazis return to their homes. An animated conversation ensued, touching on many subjects.

She told me she was in hiding during the German occupation and luckily survived with her parents and brother. This made me realize she was Jewish like me. Her name was Harriet Walvis. and I told her about my experiences, whereupon she invited me to her house for a Friday night family dinner where I'd meet her parents.

The Walvis family lived in a large, modern apartment in an affluent neighborhood of The Hague. Harriet's mother, Tillie Walvis, received me with open arms and immediately asked how to spell my last name. I complied.

"What's your mother's name?" she continued, eyes wide open.

"Leentje," I answered, surprised at the question. Then, Tillie almost stumbling screamed.

"Your mother and I are cousins. Oh God in heaven!" Then with tears in her eyes: "Were they … are they … oh God!"

This was only the first part of the result of a missed baseball pitch. It touched four people, who at the time were not aware of each other.

Harriet and I became friends and Tillie, with her husband, Harry, considered me part of the family. They included me in many of their outings and dinner parties. I had a standing invitation to the traditional Friday night Shabbat dinner.

My friend Clinton invited me to the annual Thanksgiving party to be held at the Embassy. I casually mentioned this to Harriet. She practically begged me to take her along. I asked Clinton if I could and he gave his okay. The two of them met at that party, and it was love at first sight. They got married shortly prior to the end of Clinton's tour of duty and left Holland to settle in Massachusetts. This was the second part of the missed baseball.

The third part, although insignificant, was an amazing occurrence which moved me closer to the Walvis family. They were very successful and operated several well-known ladies' clothing stores throughout The Hague. They used to go to the factories and buy clothing in bulk for cash. Then they would sell the clothes in their stores with women waiting in long lines because of the great prices and previous shortages.

Nick Walvis, Harriet's brother, was his father's right hand, and we became close friends. He had recently married a beautiful Dutch girl named Reinie, and we also grew close – almost like brother and sister. One evening I took Mary, Nick and Reinie to dine at the Hotel des Indes. It was an upscale place frequented by the diplomatic corps and government officials. While we were enjoying our meal, some bully with broad shoulders and a bulging neck stepped up to our table. He placed his big claws on the table and asked Reinie to dance, completely ignoring Nick. Reinie refused, but he insisted. I felt my rage welling up.

"Didn't you hear the lady?" I said. He then took a long look at me.

"When did you come out of hiding, little guy?" he said. The insinuation was clear, I sensed his anti-Semitism and sprang up in a blind rage.

"You son of a bitch," I yelled into his face, "I fought for you and helped liberate your country."

Then I went for him. He saw me coming and hit me hard on my chin, which made me fall back onto Reinie, who pushed me off her because she was pregnant. I bounced back fast, and my fists spun in a blur. I knocked him clear across the entire dance floor, and he ended up underneath a chair with a bloody face.

The guests in this fancy establishment looked at me in utter amazement. After a few moments of dead silence, people gave me the thumbs up. Shaking his head, Nick exclaimed, "I've never seen anybody do anything like that before!"

I suspect it might have been the extremely high income tax in Holland after the war that made difficulties for the Walvis family business. They didn't want to stay in Holland any longer. Harry Walvis made a trip around the world with his daughter Harriet and thought Brazil might be an ideal place to settle. So Nick, Reinie, Harriet and I took Portuguese lessons. I forgot why Brazil did not work out, but then Harry – this time, accompanied by his wife Tillie – went on another world trip to find a suitable place to emigrate.

Again they didn't find anything worthwhile, and on their way back to Holland, their flight was diverted to New York due to inclement weather. They didn't have U.S. visas and were not allowed off the plane. They decided not to stay in the plane until it continued back to Holland. They somehow booked a flight to Montreal, Canada, that connected with another flight directly to Holland.

As destiny would have it, Canada did not have strict visitor restrictions, and they were allowed off the plane. It was love at first sight. They stayed there for one week, had a lot of fun and loved every minute of it. They were full of stories about Montreal when they came back. It was the beauty of the city, the European atmosphere, the people and children who "were so cute with their tiny boots and parkas."

There was no doubt we were all going to Canada. Again, I hesitated; I would have to leave Mary, whom I had just started talking marriage with. But Canada bordered on the U.S., and it would get me closer to the country I really loved. I told her about my idea, and she was supportive. I promised that once I had become established in Canada, I'd send for her and we'd get married.

The third result of that missed baseball pitch was that on March 19, 1951, after some six months of filling out lengthy immigration documentation, thorough medical examinations and smallpox shots, I left Holland and emigrated to Canada. I accompanied Nick Walvis, his wife Reinie and their newly born son, Raymond. We boarded a chartered flight to Canada and arrived in Montreal at 7:40 a.m. My totally new life was about to begin, and I was one step closer to the U.S. All because of a baseball.

CHAPTER 30

A New Life in Canada

AFTER SHARING AN apartment with Nick and his family for some time, I moved out. I had been successful back in Rotterdam when we were homeless, selling men's neckties supplied by Esther's uncle; I had knocked on doors and sold out each day. So, I had the confidence to get myself a job at Tip Top Tailors on Sainte Catherine Street, the largest clothing retail store in Canada at the time. It became obvious I was skilled at sales. I worked there for over a year, was poached by another clothing store and became one of their top salesmen.

After tiring of retail, because I had to work evenings and weekends, I quit and bought my first car. For a while, I aimlessly moved around. Mary, back in Holland, and I had stopped writing to each other. I saw an ad in the newspaper looking for a sales representative with a car to represent the Enuresis Corporation of California in Ottawa and Quebec. This interested me and my sales skills got me hired immediately.

There are many children who wet their bed, a problem for both parents and kids and it causes embarrassment. A doctor in California invented a system based on Pavlov's theory, causing the child to wake up to a bell. A mat parents placed on their child's bed was connected to sensors, and when the child peed, it woke them up with an alarm. This became a game where the child learned and became conditioned to "beat the bell." It worked, and for good measure, I wore a white lab coat and rented a lot of these devices to many grateful parents.

My next foray came about because neighbors told me about a world champion skier, Tony Sailer, who was trying to sell Nordic sweaters. I saw an opportunity and grabbed the whole boatload of these high-quality items and sold a good portion to the Simpsons department store and most of the balance to a well-known discount chain store. I ended up making a pretty penny.

Nick had a family business, the Wally Trading Co., and when his father found out I had made a fortune selling ski sweaters, he got the idea to go to Hong Kong and bring back beautiful women's sequined sweaters. Then they appointed me as their sales manager for Canada.

While heading into Simpsons to make a sales presentation, I met a pretty girl named Colette who worked there. I convinced her to take her coffee break so I could talk to her in the cafeteria. She told me she was engaged to be married and a series of other complications, so I didn't think I'd see her again.

I was surprised to get a phone call from Colette about a week later, when she told me she had ran away from her fiancé and didn't get married. Colette had been taking voice lessons, and she introduced me to the world of opera, where we got to know Raoul Jobin, who later became her mentor. I learned a lot about arias, overtures and theatrical storytelling. Colette and I were married by 1957 and had a daughter, Diana. In 1958, RCA Records offered her a contract and she made the record, "*Une poupée pour Noël*." Her operatic career began to take off.

In the beginning, we temporarily lived in Colette's parents' house on Waverly Street and then moved to Place Meilleur. I should explain that I left the majority of my military documents (army discharge, flight log, medals, citations) at their house. When I went back to pick up my stuff, it was no longer there. Colette was away on tour in Europe. This happened around the time Colette and I separated and divorced. The footlocker that held so many of my important documents in neatly organized files, and my uniform stored in the basement of the home of my in-laws, went missing. Perhaps it was all thrown away by cleaners; it was not clear what happened. Luckily, my photos, documents and other army keepsakes were not inside my footlocker and were safe.

As a consequence, most of the events written in this book are derived from memory etched in my brain. No doubt errors of time, location and names have slipped into these accounts. The details of my many escapes from the Nazis did not require any research. They are burned into my memory forever.

When I was working with Nick, I met a beautiful young lady named Anne-Marie in the cafeteria of our building in 1963. It turned out she spoke Parisian French, was Jewish, was from Casablanca, Morocco, and was studying at university. She wanted to buy one of our angora sweaters, so she came up to see me in my office after finishing her work as a typist. I asked if I could drive her home.

In the car, I asked if I could take her out for dinner at my favorite authentic Chinese restaurant. She said she couldn't because she was going to volunteer at the hospital, but I convinced her to join me. After dinner we went to see the movie *My Fair Lady*, starring Audrey Hepburn. After the film, the fuzz from Anne-Marie's new angora sweater had shed and clung all over the sleeve of my silk suit from Hong Kong. From that day onward, we were together. We dated for four years – going out to dinners, dancing, parties and movies – escaping often to the Laurentians to enjoy the lakes, skiing, horseback riding and yoga. We were married by 1967. Her warm and loving family fully adopted me and taught me so much about the Jewish religion and Sephardic traditions.

When I was a manufacturer's agent on contract with Amsterdam Pen selling ballpoints to the wholesale trade, one of my clients gave me an inside tip that Aurora Plastics needed a new representative. I went after the opportunity and in no time, I became a major player in the hobby and toy business.

Eventually I was doing so well that Aurora wanted me to go to Toronto to cover the Ontario territory, and I appointed someone to cover Quebec, where I earned a good commission. When we first moved to Toronto I met up with David Koffler, whom I knew from the Wally Trading Co. in Montreal because he was their Ontario sales representative, and we became friends. By a wonderful twist of fate, he just happens to be the father of this publisher.

I now repped model cars and trains, as well as merchandise for the Hulk, Evel Knievel, *Planet of the Apes*, *Jaws*, the Invisible Man and Woman and the V8 engine model kit. Eventually, I became the hobby craft distributor to all the department stores in Canada. I had my daughter, Anna-Lea in 1968 – named after my two sisters – and my son, Jason in 1972.

My wife, Anne-Marie, had been involved in aesthetics since the 1970s and opened one of her bigger ventures, a day spa, in 1978 and then Le Minispa in 1981. Then a major supplier of mine went bankrupt, which sent me on a completely different path.

I began helping my wife with her spa business and started selling beauty equipment to salons. Eventually, I became a Chartered Life Underwriter and studied at Ryerson, obtaining my degree as a certified financial planner. I was in my sixties when I started working on Bay Street at Regal Capital Planners and sold my book almost 20 years later, finally retiring at 80.

I was grateful to be a part of the Honor flight to Washington D.C., with U.S. Army veterans out of Florida, and with Veterans Affairs Canada for the VE Day and 80th Anniversary of the Liberation of the Netherlands – a weeklong celebration in Toronto. I also was honored to receive the Ontario Seniors Achievement Award for my efforts to share my story and spread awareness of how hate can breed violence.

Parents, their children, and people of all ages and walks of life who attend my talks at schools, synagogues, legions, churches and companies have often asked what message I have in the event of another Holocaust, which, in my opinion is a very likely possibility. I ask them: "What would *you* have done, when at age 16, all your rights were taken away?"

In answer to what made me do the things I did, the answer is simple. Most of my escapes were not planned. They were motivated by fear and the will to survive – the greatest motivators. I consider myself to be extremely lucky, and I don't understand, out of all my friends and family, why I was the only one to have survived.

My message is clear: "Stand up for your rights as a human being; let no one take away your birthright. Fight for it if necessary. To defend it is the cost of freedom."

About the Author

JACK BOEKI was born on May 31, 1924, in Rotterdam, Netherlands, and grew up in a non-religious Jewish family. After his war exploits, Jack worked in Hong Kong before moving to Canada in 1951, where he worked in sales, as an entrepreneur and as a financial advisor in Toronto. In recognition of Jack's engagement in community life, at the age of 101, he received the 2024 Ontario Senior's Achievement Award. His life reflects extraordinary resilience, courage, and dedication to remembrance and education.